How to

Raise a

Superhero

Joe Grutzik

First Printing: 2018

ISBN 978-0-9768915-5-0

Good & Brown Publishing
1162 Chestnut Ave.

Manhattan Beach CA 90266

www.goodandbrown.com

To my fantastic father

John Francis Grutzik

The original Superdaddy

Contents

PREFACE

I'm kind of a typical guy, about average height, about
average weight. I grew up in the 70's as the middle kid in a
family of five. I was a cute, dumb, clumsy kid with below
average athletic ability.

We lived in a normal house in the middle of the street in
the center of a neighborhood in a suburb of Los Angeles in the
middle of Southern California. My mom was a part-time
substitute teacher. My dad was an aerospace engineer. We
lived in a nice, middle-class suburb on a nice, wide street with
a bunch of nice families, whose dads all seemed to be
engineers working for the space program. My dad was a quiet
man of few words. My mom was a loud lady with a lot of
energy.

We looked like a middle-class family of medium income,
but we were always broke. My mom and dad had five kids in
eight years, one right after the next. To feed all the kids and
run our household on my father's modest income my parents
ran a very tight budget. And they were very good at not
spending any money.

Because my mom and dad had lived through tough times
when there was no stuff and no money they were really good
at scrimping and saving. Most of our clothes came from
second-hand stores and all of my clothes were hand-me-downs

that my mother had bought for my brother from thrift shops, hand-me-downs of hand-me-downs.

Our house was loud, crazy and violent. My mother used fear and intimidation to try to control her rambunctious kids. Her favorite strategy to keep us in line was to pit the kids against each other so that she didn't have to do all the beating. If one of us got too loud or out of line, she would tell my older brother to take care of it. And he loved nothing more than torturing one of his younger siblings.

Being the middle kid in the family, I was the needy, insecure goofball. I was loud and braggadocios. I was the tallest kid in class but always the slowest. My younger sisters were cute and pretty. My older sister was smart. My mom loved my older brother the best, and I was stuck in the middle.

I wasn't really bright enough to figure out school. I was the class clown, the troublemaker in the back, the guy that was always looking for a way to blow things up. I was caustically compelled to act out. Overcompensating for being stuck in the middle, I was the kid that had to take a fall or tell a joke to get attention.

Growing up I never felt secure. I never felt safe. I was always off balance. I had no foundation. I had no place to stand. The ground under my feet was constantly quivering like a landfill in an earthquake.

From a very early age, I knew I wanted to have kids. I wanted to have a family. I knew I wanted to have kids, but I didn't want to have kids and then put them through the kind of crap that I went through when I was growing up.

I wanted to have a family, but I wanted to have a better family. I wanted to do a better job than my mom and dad did.

I guess that is pretty normal. I guess that is the typical thing that the typical guy wants to do. He wants to do a little bit better than his mom and dad did.

But I'm not your typical dad.

I had trouble in school, so I left and went skiing. I was a ski bum for about ten years before I woke up and realized that this was kind of a dumb way to live. Life was too easy.

So I went back to school. I graduated from the University of Arizona with an engineering degree. I was ten years older than most of the other kids in my class.

So early in life, I had a mix and jumble of two very different lifestyles. I spent ten years as an international vagabond ski bum, and then I went back to school to study calculus. This experience taught me to think in two very different ways. The first way was kind of the hipster/beat/philosopher. With time on my hands, I read a lot of Nietzsche.

The second life was more pragmatic. As an engineer, you learn how to see base reality with logic, reason and cold hard facts. Engineers see the world in a very different way than normal people. They have to deal with the real world. Engineers have to understand the fundamentals of reality for what it really is. They have to do this because they need to design reliable products like cars and airplanes. Engineers need to design and build stuff that doesn't break. They need to understand base reality because if they don't do their job right and they build stuff that breaks, people die.

So I went back to school. I went back to school because I wanted to do something hard. Engineering was hard so that fit into the plan. Around the same time, I got married. I knew that marriage was hard so I thought, at the time, that this would be a good plan, doing two really hard things at the same time.

I got married to a very smart woman. She also decided to go back to school to get her Ph.D. from UCLA.

When my wife decided that she wanted to start trying to have kids, she was very sweet about it. She made a little ceremony out of the asking. She made me a special present. She brought me into the kitchen of our one-bedroom apartment and she gave me a small box. In the box was a gold chain necklace. On the chain was a small golden figure. The figure on the chain was kind of like the 30,000-year-old Venus figure of a pregnant mother.

I knew instantly what she was trying to say. I knew what she meant, and I knew what she wanted.

I winced.

I was scared and I wasn't ready. I hadn't matured. Or, better, I hadn't evolved. I was still greedy and selfish. I hadn't yet grown through Maslow's Hierarchy of Needs.

I was working at a job that I hated trying to make enough money to do something spectacular. I wanted more. I wasn't ready to have kids. I wanted to have gotten something important done. I wanted to be more successful and established. I figured that once we started having kids it was over. My life as I knew it was finished. I didn't want to bring another life into this world before I was done with mine. I wasn't done yet. And I felt like I hadn't done enough.

Have you ever felt that way?

Looking back I realize that I hadn't taken the time to define my values, and I had adopted trivial, shallow, media-driven goals.

I never asked myself about purpose. I don't think I had ever really thought about life that way. I had things that I wanted to do. I had an idea, a vision really, about what an exciting life would look like. I had done a lot of exciting things and I had this idea that I wanted to do a lot more exciting things.

At the center of all of this was "I".

I was at the center of everything. I wasn't really aware of any other way to think about life. I had been building my life on a set of experiences, a list of things that I wanted to accomplish; I hadn't ever thought that there might be a better way to organize a life.

Have you ever wondered about stuff like this?

Have you ever asked yourself -

What is my purpose?

Or -

Why am I here?

Have you ever thought that it might be a good idea to write down your values? And then maybe design your purpose around your values?

I hadn't.

I was flying by the seat of my pants. I didn't plan; I improvised, to me that was the most exciting way to live. It is exciting but it gets really sketchy. When you don't plan things out you can end up running down dead ends or painting yourself into a corner.

I was running full speed, around blind corners, dumping paint into dead ends, not slowing for a moment to wonder why. I had never really asked where I was going, what road I was on or where that road was headed.

I had never asked myself if I should even be chasing after all of the stuff that I was chasing. What was that stuff? Did I really want that stuff? Was that stuff ever going to bring me happiness or fulfillment?

I didn't see it at the time but I was setting myself up for a huge crash, a big disaster.

So why write this book? What is this book about? What compels a sixty-year-old guy to stop and write a book about raising children?

I'm writing this book because I wanted to tell other guys what I know. I thought that if I could share my experiences I might be able to save other fathers from the pain and suffering of making a major mistake.

I want to help other fathers not make the same mistakes that I have made.

I wanted to teach fathers what I have learned.

I see guys struggle with their position and place and purpose, and I wanted to share a different point of view.

I see a lot of dads bumbling around looking like they don't know what they're doing. They don't know how to be a dad. And that hurts me. As an empathetic human, I feel their pain. I figure that if I could just give them a few pointers I could make their lives so much easier.

So I started to write this. I started with my understanding that –

the cornerstone of society
is the family
and the foundation of the family is
fatherhood.

When we had our first child, I had no idea what I was doing. I read a bunch of books. Some of them were good, but most of them were like cook books. They talked about how to do stuff. Put in some of this and then put in some of that and then do this and then do that. That's great. Everybody needs an owner's manual. But that's not what this book is about. As the hipster/beat/philosopher/engineer, I wanted to know the answers to deeper questions.

I wanted to know stuff like:

How could I take a fragile loaf of phlegm and help it develop into a powerful, charismatic, empathetic human?

How do I teach my kids to be strong-willed but also kind?

How do I teach my kids to be self-reliant and independent and at the same time keep them rooted in family and committed to culture and community?

How can I teach my kids to lead full and exciting lives and teach them that 90% of limitations are self-imposed and that they are only as free as they think they are?

How can I raise cool, calm and peaceful kids that know how to dance?

How can I guide their lives in a positive direction and away from negative, violent situations?

And how can I do this better than my mom and dad did?

That is what this book is about.
These are the kinds of questions that I answer in this book.
It took me more than 20 years to figure this out.
It is still a work in progress and I still have time to mess it up, but here is what I've learned. Here is what I know. And here is what I am going to share with you.

This book is not just the how but the why.

This book is about not just being a dad but being a purposeful parent.

This book is about how to become a Superdaddy so that you can raise superhero kids.

But wait –

There is more.

If you are patient with me, if you stick around to the end,
I might tell you more.

I might tell you the whats and the whys.

What is our purpose?

Why are we here?

Why have kids?

What is the point?

What is the reason that we do all of this?

Why should we choose life?

Why live?

And maybe, just maybe:

What is the meaning of life?

Section 1

THE BEGINNING

It was another bright, sunny, clear morning.

Like every other bright, sunny, clear weekday morning in Eagle Rock, California.

I was your typical mild-mannered stay-at-home dad working as a technical sales consultant for a high-tech remote sensing company based in Colorado.

My life was cake.

Like every other weekday morning, I was moving through my daily routine. I would wake up early and make a pot of coffee. Then I would bring my wife a cup and wake our two small children. I would get them dressed and make everybody breakfast.

When they were ready, I would help the whole crew down to the car and strap the kids into their car seats. My wife would usually drop the kids off at daycare on her way to work, and I would pick them up in the afternoon.

I would kiss everybody goodbye and head back upstairs to start my day. I would usually make a second pot of coffee, flip on the TV and catch up on the news.

But today was different.

I filled the kettle and put it on the burning stove. Then I poured some beans into the grinder as an image appeared on the muted television.

Something was wrong. What was usually Matt Lauer and the Today show looked like the preview for a new superhero action movie. The lower half of Manhattan was engulfed in a huge post-apocalyptic cloud of toxic debris. I thought it must have been a commercial for the next Spider-Man flick.

I ground the beans and poured the dust into the maker. Then I walked across the room and grabbed the remote.

The scene hadn't changed. It was just one live, long shot of Lower Manhattan. This wasn't right. Some huge disaster must have happened in Lower Manhattan. I didn't know what it was, but I knew it was big. I made a dash for the door and ran back downstairs to try and catch my wife before she took off. I wanted her to come back upstairs and look at the news, but it was too late. She was already on her way.

Panicked, I ran back upstairs to the television. It was still just that long, low, wide shot of the dust cloud over Manhattan. And there was something else wrong.

What? What is that? The Twin Towers are gone. There was nothing on the skyline where the twin towers should be. That can't be real. That can't be Manhattan.

I changed the channel, flipping over to another network, and un-muted the TV.

"Here is what we know so far. The first plane crashed into the North Tower of the World Trade Center at 8:46 am Eastern Standard Time."

I said to myself, "The first plane? There was more than one plane?"

"The second plane hit the WTC South Tower at 9:03 am. We are going to show a replay of the second plane hitting the building. Do we have that tape? This is a replay from our NBC affiliate in New York City."

I watched an airplane fly into one of the Twin Towers, and huge flames exploded out from the other side of the building.

I felt sick.

"We're hearing now that there seems to be smoke coming from the Pentagon. We have unconfirmed reports that this was the result of a plane crashing in the area. My colleague, who just came in … it appears that whatever it was, and perhaps it was a plane, if those are the initial reports, crashed into—at the heliport side of the Pentagon, which is just opposite of the Potomac River."

I thought, Three Planes? This is an organized attack.
"At 9:59 am the South Tower of the World Trade Center collapsed followed by the North Tower at 10:28 am."
I watched a replay of the first tower falling. I instinctively knew that tens of thousands of people worked at the World Trade Center.

I remember thinking to myself,
Where was Superman?
Where are the superheroes?
Where is the Navy or the Marines?
Where is the Army or the Airforce?
What the hell is going on?
How could they let this happen?
Where was Superman?

Then, suddenly, from somewhere inside our house there was a loud scream.

I nearly jumped out of my pants.

It was just my tea kettle.

It had come to boil.

I know that I won't be alone in saying that that moment changed my life.
That was the singular most catastrophic thing that had ever happened to me.
In that moment my view of reality was fractured. The looking glass cracked. It took a while for each of the reflective pieces of reality to fall and an even longer time for me to discover a newer truth, a clearer reflection of reality. But that is when it all began.
At that moment I felt vulnerable and scared. I felt inadequate and unprotected.

At first, it was just a shock to my schema, my view of reality. It was like I woke up and realized that the world was a lot more complicated and a lot more violent than I had thought.

And then I felt scared for my kids. We had led a relatively happy and carefree life until that time. I hadn't thought very much about the future or defense or what we would do if something went wrong because up to that point nothing had really ever gone wrong.

After a few days, I really started to freak out. I couldn't sleep. I couldn't really even lie in bed.

We had little savings, no life insurance, not very much money and no back-up plan.

Things were bad and seemed to be getting worse all the time.

I wondered what we would do if things really went south. What would happen to my family? What would happen to my kids? They are so young. Who would protect them? What would they do?

The events of 9/11 started me on a long journey. It was the impetus, the spark that got me going and made me re-evaluate my life. It made me begin to ask the deeper questions about life—why we are here, what our purpose is and what we are doing.

I spent the next couple years floundering around. It took me that long to process what had happened. It took me that long to readjust and broaden my world view. It took about two years to come to terms with this new reality and make a plan. But then, after a while, I settled down and got to work.

This book is about part of that journey, part of that quest.

From that quest, along that path, fighting my way through that toxic debris cloud, I found some of the answers that I had started looking for so many years ago.

One of those answers is about purpose, family, and fatherhood.

I've written this book in part to answer the questions: Where is Superman? Where are the superheroes? Where are the people that we need to step in in the moment of crisis and save the world?

This book is about how to be a dad—how to be a good dad and why the family is important.

I have realized that most dads just don't know what they are doing. They don't have the basics down. They don't have the most basic common understanding of what it means to be a dad, why they are a father or what the purpose of the family is.

So I thought I would write some of this down to talk about the basics.

This book is about the how: how not to be just your mild-mannered, regular dad but how to reach the highest order of dad you can be. How you can be a Superdaddy.

What are the rules? What are the lessons? What are the tricks to raising superheroes?

Most chapters start with a story of where I was and what I was doing when I learned the lesson. Some of these lessons I learned under extreme duress in a painful circumstance. Some of these examples I tested on my own kids. I present my best lessons here so that you won't have to slog through the muck and the pain; you won't have to solve the problem yourself. You can just learn from my experience.

Some of the chapters give specific instructions and action steps that you can take today to make your parenting more successful. And some of these actions can give you real-life Superpowers.

Let's get started.

What is the most powerful force in the universe?

Is it gravity?

Is it entropy?

Would you like to be able to control the most powerful force in the universe?

LESSON ONE

Love and horse manure

I first heard of this idea from Scott Peck in The Road Less Traveled. My soon to be wife and I read this book together on a road trip once. To me the idea made sense. The story goes something like this.

People love all kinds of things. Some guys love cars; some guys love to watch football; some guys like to garden. Well, it turns out that there is a pretty good positive correlation between the things you spend time doing and the things you love.

Let's say you love to garden. What is a garden? A garden starts out as a big pile of horse manure. You get a big pile of poo and you dump it in the middle of your yard. Every day you spend a couple hours working on your plot. You plan out your garden and mark off the land. You till the droppings into the soil. You level the ground and trowel the soil into rows. You collect the seeds and design the layout. You plant and water. For every action and every hour you invest in your garden, your love for the garden grows. You don't start out loving a big pile of horse dung. You work your way into it.

The more you work in your garden, the more you will love your garden. The more effort you put into it, the more you will anticipate the harvest. The harder you work on it, the more value you place on it.

This meme is a natural human trait, and this idea applies to everything you do. The longer you watch the NFL, the more you love football. The more you work on your car, the more you love your car. The more you play video games, the more you love video games. And it's not just the thing that you love; it's the part of you that you have committed and invested in the thing. You place a value on it and the thing that you value is the time that you've invested. That time has value and you cherish that time.

It becomes very important to purposely pick the things that you love. Direct your attention towards powerful things. Pick your passions and don't let your attentions be scattered willy-nilly. Don't, for instance, start watching some TV sitcom just because it happens to be the thing that's on every day when you get home from work. You'll watch a couple episodes just because it's on and you're tired and hungry, but pretty soon it's a habit. Then every day you'll find yourself watching the same stupid TV show. After a while, you'll start loving "your shows." You'll forget the fact that they are just stupid drivel. You'll love your shows and you won't know why. You will be blinded to the fact that these shows are a stupid, brain-sucking waste of your life.

Pick the passions that can be applied with leverage. Take a moment to choose the things that will make a difference in what you do, and pick the things that you can get better at. For instance, make a list of the things that you're interested in. Let's say you want to make a change and you want to move your life in a different direction. Make a list of the things that you're curious about. Let's say that on that list you have the LA Lakers, helicopters, and the stock market. Well, let's say you pick the LA Lakers. You love the Lakers and you want to learn more about them. You're a fan but you really enjoy watching the Lakers and you want to become a super fan. Well, look down the road a bit and tell me what you see. How will that change you? Where will that lead? How good of a fan can you become? I mean, you can only go so far with that. It will only take you to a certain point. You can only get so good at being a fan and then—what?

And then nothing—it really hasn't given you anything but a few hours of diversion and wasted time. Oh sure, you had fun while you were doing it, but has watching someone else play a game really done you any lasting good or made you a better person? It is more important to pick a fecund passion. Purposely pick a passion that has a payoff. Pick something that through time and study can make you and the world better off. Pick a passion that will take a lot of time and a lot of work. Plant a garden that you can work at, watch grow and reap the harvest.

So back to love—love is an action. The more effort and work you focus on the object of your love, the more you will love the object. This is true for your car, your team, your garden, your wife, and your kids.

If you want to love your wife, love your wife. Show your wife love and attention. Work on it. Find things that you can do for her every day and all of the time that will make her life easier and better. Take action. Anticipate her needs and wants. Support her pursuits. Do things for her, all of the time. Your relationship with your wife is like anything else: the harder you work on it, the more you will love it. The more affection and attention you give your wife, the more love you will generate within your relationship.

And it's the same with your kids. Love your kids. Pay attention. This attention is a focus. Be present while spending time with your kids. You might be watching something else or doing something else while you're spending time with your kids, but make sure that you are there with them and that they are the primary focus of your attention. Engage with them on a deeper level, a more fundamental level than whatever secondary action or focus you're engaged in.

The more attention and affection you give to your kids, the more you will love your kids and the more they will love you.

And if you feel that your wife doesn't love you enough or that your kids are drifting away, stop and turn around. You can't take more from your garden than you've planted. You have to stop and refocus on giving more than you get. You have to put more effort, attention, and affection into the relationship or situation. The more work you do in your garden, the more you will love it and the better it will be.

What is the most powerful force in the universe?

Is it gravity?

Is it entropy?

Would you like to be able to control the most powerful force in the universe?

Love is a verb.

Love is an action.

Get to work.

Superpower #1

LOVE

Understanding this one simple meme gives you the power to act.

It changes your strategic position from a reactive pawn on the chess board of human relationships to an active participant and directive leader in that game space.

Let's talk for a moment about the difference between active and reactive strategies.

In every situation—be it human interaction, conflicts with your environment, or conflicts within your own mind—it is better to take action.

In any situation, you can either be the active participant, the operator that makes a plan in the pursuit of a goal and then executes his plan, or you can be the reactive participant, the subject that is constantly reacting to what other operators are doing.

This is true in every conversation, every situation and every interaction with every other person you will ever meet.

You can either have a plan in pursuit of a goal or something that you want—be the one that takes action, makes a directive, executes a plan and makes movement disrupting the status quo—or you can constantly react to what other players, influences, pressures, and people are doing.

If you are constantly reacting, you don't have a plan.

If you are constantly reacting, you don't have a goal.

If you are constantly reacting, you don't know what you want in life; you don't have a purpose.

If you are constantly reacting, you are always on your heels. You are always stressed out. You are always tired. You are always depressed.

If you are purposely and positively pursuing the object of your desire, you are in control. You dictate the direction of others, you are the operator, and you move and control the reactors.

Taking action is always preferable to reacting to what others do.

The best defense is always a good offense.

Because you are taking action and making other players react to your moves.

If you are continually taking action in the pursuit of the object of your desire, you are always in a ready stance, on the balls of your feet. You have all the positive energy. You are calm and relaxed because you know where you're going. You are happy and energized.

And there is more.

It's time to level up -

Let's turn this back to the idea of love.

If you are in love with someone and you are wanting for that person to love you, you are reacting to their action.

Sure, it feels good to be in love. But that feeling will only last for about two weeks. And then you will start to feel tired, lonely, stressed out and depressed.

By simply understanding the meme that love is an action, it changes the paradigm. It gives you a framework, a scaffolding, a way to take action.

It gives you a Superpower.

It gives you the Superpower of Superpowers.

It gives you the Superpower of Love, the most powerful force in the universe.

By intentionally performing positive, helpful activities for the people that are close to you, you are controlling the game space.

With this Superpower, you have Unlimited Energy, Superhuman Strength, and Superhuman Endurance.

Love is the most powerful Superpower you can possibly have.

So, Superpower #1 is:

Love

Develop this Superpower first.

Choose your values.

Find your purpose.

Make a plan.

Take action.

Move with purpose, using your values as a guide, in the direction of your goal.

Make the world a better place –

by making better children.

What is better than having money in the bank?

You have a minimum balance, but what is better?

Leverage

Leverage is the ability to borrow more money.

Leverage is more important than money.

Would you like to have more leverage?

LESSON TWO

The Love Bank

So, as your kids grow through their middle years, between the ages of three and 12 they pretty much just want to play. But when they get to like 13, 14, 15, things start to change. This is when their hormones start kicking in.

When your kids get into seventh grade, it's like their brain explodes and they become aware of a lot of other things that are going on around them. There are a lot of social interactions that go on between people that children don't ever see. There is a constant battle going on between people all the time. This battle is just under the tongue or just barely subliminal. Adults are judging people and grading each other all the time. They might do it right out in the open or they might not even realize they do it. But it's happening and kids don't notice it. Their brains aren't big enough yet to make the connections.

But once they get a little older and their brains develop in a certain way, they suddenly see these Playground Politics going on around them and it freaks them out. It happens first with little girls. Little girls develop an understanding of social interaction several years before boys do. That is just how it is. Little girls are just better connected. And once they get into seventh grade, their brains explode; they begin to realize that other people are talking about them and other little girls are thinking about them and they really freak out.

You'll need to be ready for this. You will need to have your foundations set and strong before this time comes. You'll need to have your relationships solid with your children before this change happens. You'll need to have your Love Bank full before you get to this point. Because once they hit this point, once their brain wakes up and they begin to intuit what others are thinking, their entire world view changes and you will no longer be walking around in the same world. Your kid and especially your daughter will suddenly rearrange her priorities, and your place in her hierarchy of important and valuable people, her Org Chart, will suddenly shift.

You will pick her up from school one day, and she will be either sobbing in tears or mad as hell. She will go on and on about a girl that said something about her or her group of girlfriends that she has been friends with since second grade suddenly rejected her and now she is poison. No one will talk to her and no one will be her friend.

This rejection will now become the most important, highest priority issue in her life. Not her school work. Not her volleyball. Not her family and not you.

From that moment on, all bets are off. Her mind will be made up and you will not be changing her mind.

The most interesting part of this is—it is now that she has her own mind. This is the point where she makes a huge leap, where her brain has developed, where she becomes a bigger person, where she becomes more fully human, and, like I said before if you don't have your foundations set by this point, you run the risk of losing her. You will have less influence. You will have less leverage. You will be able to provide less guidance, and it will be more difficult to guide her away from these smaller distractions in life and help her set her priorities on bigger things.

So, I need to talk about the Love Bank.

What is the Love Bank?

Like I have said many times, I believe that love is an action. I know, I know there are many different definitions of love, but most of those other definitions are poetic, romantic, pornographic, or poppycock that bring no value. These other definitions of love talk about feelings and emotions and motives and descriptions of things that happened to you in the past. None of these other definitions give you actionable information, a strategy to employ, an action to take, a path to follow to make relationships better, to make your life better, to make you a better lover and to actually make love better.

The most important definition of love is this;

Love is a verb.
Love is an action.
Love is what you do.

So if you want someone to love you, you need to DO something for them. Let's say that you have been in a relationship for a while. You began this relationship with all the poppycock feelings that I mentioned above. Your feelings and emotions for this person were poetic and romantic. Your lust for this person was real and overwhelming. You felt complete when you were around this person and you just wanted to always be near them.

Well, that's great. But now what are you going to do to make this relationship healthy and happy and strong? What are you going to do to make this partnership last?

This definition gives you the answer. Love is an action. So take action. Do something for this person to show them that you love them. Think every day, "What can I do today to make my partner's life a little better?" It could be a big thing like fixing their car or mowing their lawn. It could be something minor like cooking her dinner, doing a load of laundry or cleaning up after yourself. Or it could be something silly like bringing them a cup of coffee or putting the seat down. But the more you can do to make her life a little better today, the more Love you will give and the more love you will get.

You want to show your partner that you are thinking about them, that you hold them in high esteem. That you

35

value them as a person, as a partner, and as a lover and you place them near the top of the things that you value. You don't put them fourth or fifth on your Org Chart. This is like that scene in Spider-Man where Spider-Man has to choose between saving the gondola full of strangers or saving the life of his girlfriend. If you have a date with your partner and your friends or your boss call you on that night and ask you to go out, you tell them no. You blow them off and you go out with your partner. This is the way you show your partner and your boss and your friends that you value your partner more than you value them. This is the way you organize your Org Chart. You organize your Org Chart so that you can see your Org Chart so that your partner can see your Org Chart and so that the rest of the world can see your Org Chart by the actions that you take.

It is important to understand that this is not about what you say. What you say has very little meaning. I don't care about what a person says to me. I judge a person by his actions. If a guy says he is going to do something and he does it, that's golden. If a guy says one thing and then does something else, then that guy cannot be trusted. You can tell a girl you love them every day, but to me, that doesn't mean very much. You have to show the girl that you love her by doing things for her every day. That has meaning. That is important. That is golden.

So what does this have to do with the Love Bank?

The Love Bank is a virtual account of all these little actions that you take to show your partner that you love them. From the moment you start your relationship, you put little things, actions, gifts, batches of bread, presents, time, favors, backrubs, dinners on the town, breakfasts in bed, help with their homework, rides to school, random acts of kindness and everything else you do for that person into a virtual account. You don't need to keep track of this account. The other person will subconsciously keep track. But you do need to keep filling it up. You need to make a deposit in the Love Bank every day.

It is important to know that the balance goes up and down in the Love Bank. Sometimes you will need a favor from a friend or your partner and it will be a very big deal. This one favor might be worth more than all the other trivial acts that you have done to build the balance in your account. This is a withdrawal from the Love Bank, and you don't want to get into a situation where you have insufficient funds. You want to keep your balance high. You want to keep a high minimum balance.

You can see this in relationships all the time. You can see relationships in which one partner takes and takes and takes—they make withdrawals all the time. They never give back. They never make a deposit. They just take and take until their account is completely overdrawn and the other person in the partnership is empty. These relationships go on way too long and usually end badly. These relationships end badly because one of the people in the partnership doesn't take action; he doesn't treat love as an action. He doesn't make deposits in the Love Bank and he doesn't keep his balance above the minimum balance.

So, where do kids fit in? How do you and why should you keep a high balance in your account in your Love Bank with your kids? This is a very big deal. This is one of the most important strategies you can employ to build successful relationships with your kids. Here is how it works.

The path to a happy, healthy relationship with your children is very, very difficult and dangerous. The path is very, very long and for the first 20 years or so, the path is all uphill. At times the path gets treacherous. It will be raining and cold at 3 am and you might be running on little food and less sleep. You know in the back of your mind that your day's journey has just begun and you have a long, long road ahead of you. You know that you will need everything you have to get through this, and you will need help from your partner and your kids. (This is not a hypothetical case. This was a typical Saturday morning getting ready to go to a volleyball tournament.)

This is the time you need your kids to trust you. You need them to do what you say. At times like this, you will need to have a huge balance in your Love Bank. You will need this balance because you might need to draw this balance down to zero today just to get through the day.

This is why you start early. This is why you add big Love deposits to your child's Love Bank starting from day one. Every day, from the first moment you see your baby, you love them and hold them. Every day of their lives you cook for them and clean up after them. For the first year, you are constantly feeding them and wiping the sticky, gumming baby poo off the back of their car seat. Every day for the first three years you are holding them until your arms hurt and listening to baby gibberish in a language you barely know. Every day for the first five years, you are holding them and kissing them and finding things to teach them so that they learn that learning is the most important thing they can do. Every day for the first 10 years, you are blowing off your boss and your friends to show your kid that they are number 3 on your Org Chart. And every day you are holding them and loving them and putting huge Love deposits into the Love Bank so that when the time comes for you to have influence, when the time comes when they are fragile and torn apart by raging hormones and Playground Politics, you have leverage, you have purchase, you have a balance in the Love Bank, and your child knows that they can trust you and maybe listen to what you say.

You start early and you make massive, endless deposits into the Love Bank accounts of your children so that when your daughter turns 14 in seventh grade and gets in the car bawling her eyes out about some insignificant, minor infraction that one of her ex-best friends did to her –

You can talk to her –

And she will listen to you.

This one moment will be worth more than all the money that you will ever make.

And this will pay off in ways that you cannot imagine.

Keep a massively high minimum balance in your Love Bank.

Superpower #2

Influence

Let's say that you are a businessman with a small muffler shop in a small town in the middle of Montana. Let's say that you have been doing business in that small town for 10 years. Let's say that every workday for the last 10 years you have gone to the bank to make a deposit. The teller knows your name. The manager knows your name and the bank president knows your name. The bank knows what your minimum balance has been and knows what your average daily deposit is. The bank also knows if any of their other customers are pissed off at you and they know if you are pissed off at anyone else.

Basically, the bank knows you and knows how you are as a businessman.

Then one day you have an idea. You want to open another shop in the next town. You want to open another shop, but you don't quite have enough cash to carry the two shops through the first six months of operations. What do you do?

First of all, you know that you never borrow money for a personal item like a car or a boat or a TV. You only borrow money for an investment in which the rate of return on the investment is greater than the operating costs, including the interest on the loan.

After you run the numbers to make sure that you think this can work, you go to your bank and ask them for a loan. And the bank knows you. They've seen how hard you work. They know what kind of person you are and they know what you are capable of doing. They know what your minimum balance has been for the last ten years. So, they give you the loan.

This is the way it is with all personal relationships. You work hard every day. You make a deposit in the Love Bank every day. You keep a high minimum balance in the Love Bank every day. And when you go to make a withdrawal, you know you've got capital to cover the withdrawal.

But you are not a just a guy with a muffler shop in Montana (well, maybe you are but anyway); you are a Superdaddy. How does this apply to you? What Superpower does this provide?

This provides the Superpower of Influence. You are not just taking a withdrawal from the bank. You are taking a withdrawal with leverage. You are taking a loan. You are putting capital to use. You are using your personal credit history and your personal reputation, credibility, and trust to spend in excess of what your balance is. People know you and trust you. They have seen what you've done in the past and they know what you are capable of.

This is the Superpower. It is love again, just like the first Superpower, but it is love with interest. It is love with leverage. This Superpower is influence. If you take the time and put in the effort required to obtain this Superpower, you will have influence over the people that you love. When you talk, they will listen. When they need advice, they will come to you.

This influence will become a power many multiples of what any standard mild-mannered man might have.

If you obtain this Superpower, you will be able to help and coach and advise dozens, hundreds or even thousands of people.

It is a huge Superpower.

It is the Superpower of influence.

To earn the Superpower, grow and maintain large minimum balances in the Love Banks of every person that you know. This effort and investment will come back to you ten thousand fold.

If you could give your children anything, what would you give them?

Would you give them money?

Would you give them success?

Would you give them happiness?

Or would you give them something more?

Something that is more foundational. Something that, when applied, could lead to money, success, and happiness?

If you could, would you give your children a bigger and more powerful sense of self?

Would you like to give your children a foundation of emotional security?

LESSON THREE

Love'em

We were living in a small one-bedroom apartment in West Los Angeles somewhat close to the UCLA campus. My wife was pregnant, and I was trying to start a new business. I was taking the bus up to see her. I don't remember why I was taking the bus. But I remember that I had a backpack and a bundle of flowers. It was the middle of the afternoon and the bus was kind of empty. At one of the stops, a homeless guy got on. He was one of these old guys in his sixties that never bathed and wore all the clothing he owned. With a big, long coat on top of two or three filthy hoodie sweatshirts, a sticky gray beard, long filthy fingernails and a pungent odor.

He climbed aboard the bus and took a seat next to me. Well, he smelled bad. Bad enough for the two or three passengers near us to get up and move to the back of the bus. For some reason, I just thought that I would stay where I was, next to him, in the otherwise empty front of the bus. I didn't want to move. A) I was kind of curious. I wondered what this guy was like. You never really get a chance to intermingle with such a divergent personality, and I was wondering if I could gain any insight into his life. And B) I didn't want to react. I wanted to see what would happen.

I didn't get up. I just sat there. And we didn't say anything.

After a couple stops, the guy turns to me and asks, "Are you okay?" I was like, "Excuse me?" He said, "What's wrong? What's the matter? You don't look well."

I was kind of knocked back. This wasn't what I thought might happen. It was outside of my construct. I didn't know what to say, so I ended up saying whatever was first in my mental queue.

"Oh, ah, I guess I am stressed out. My wife's pregnant with our first child and I just quit my job. I'm starting a new business and having a kid is kind of freaking me out."

He said, "Oh, don't worry. Everything will be OK."

I kind of laughed and asked, "Really, how do you know?"

He said, "Oh, I know. I've had kids. I know about these things."

I was stunned. I didn't really expect to be talking to this guy. I didn't expect a homeless man to be giving me worldly advice, today, on a bus, driving through Los Angeles.

Then he said, "You know about kids? I know about kids. I know the secret to raising happy children."

I looked at him again. Here was a strange old man in the middle of the city, beaten by life, living on the street. What had he been through? What the hell did he know? It was weird. I felt chills. This guy looked like a Jedi Master, like an apparition, like Obi-Wan Kenobi stepping into my life to tell me something important. It was eerie.

I said, "What's that? What's the secret? What's the secret to raising happy children?"

He said, "All's you have to do is love them. I mean really love them. I mean deep down. You have to love them. You have to let them know that they are loved. You have to hold them every chance you get because you might not get another chance. You have to squeeze them tight and keep them safe."

At this point, I could see that the old man was crying. "You just have to love them..." This simple statement cracked me. The old man looked directly into my eyes and finished, "... every chance you get."

I choked up and started to cry.

The bus came to a stop and the old sage got up and stepped off. He didn't turn or wave. He just got off and stood there with his back to us and his head down as the bus pulled away.

I never forgot that. I felt like this stranger came into my life for a reason. And that this was a simple but important lesson to remember.

Love your baby.

I took his advice seriously. I held my babies as long as I could, every day. And I learned while I was doing this that something magical happens when you hold your baby. It is really magic when you love your kids. I mean really love them. There's something about holding your baby and keeping it safe. There is something magical about squeezing your baby tight. They respond like magic. It makes them feel safe and secure. It makes a big difference.

A father should hold his baby every day—for as long as he can. And squeeze him or her tight. Look into their eyes, close and secure, nose to nose, and tell them you love them. It makes your baby feel secure and it changes the way they grow.

Do this every day, all the time.

You want to bond with your child. Like a mamma gorilla bonds with her baby. You want to hold your baby as long as you can, every day. In a perfect world, you will hold or carry your child in your arms or on your body all day long. You hold them while you sit, you stay with them while they're taking a nap and you tie them into a sling or a pouch on your body while you're working. You try to do this every day, all the time for at least the first six months.

In the wild a mamma gorilla physically holds her baby in her arms or on her body continually, 24 hours a day, for a half a year. She does this to keep her baby safe in a hostile environment. I believe that these mammalian familiar procedures are hardwired into our brains. And as for the gorilla, the chimpanzee, the baboon and many other large primates, these practices trigger deeply rooted feelings and emotions in the baby and the mother and father. In turn, these actions change the way the baby's mind develops. The baby develops knowing that she is safe and cared for. And her mind and brain grow and change in accordance with her environment.

If you think about it, you really don't get that many chances to hold your baby. From the time they are born until the time they become physically too big to carry, you might get only two thousand chances to hold your child in your arms. That's 365 days/year until they are five years old. That's not much time. It is a brief window. It is open for a while and then it's gone. It only happens two thousand times. And you should take every advantage, every time, to hold your baby.

This is the most important thing you can do for your child. It makes them feel safe. It makes them feel secure. This security percolates all the way down to the very bottom of their soul. This security enables your baby's brain to develop in a completely different way.

This action, this simple habit, builds a fundamental bond between you and your children that can never be broken. Hold your child every day. And every day you will build a connection with your child like nothing you have ever known.

Think about the things you can give your children.
You can give them money.

You can hand them success.

You can help them to be happy.

You can give them all of that and more.

You can give your children emotional security and a bigger, more powerful sense of self by holding your baby every day.

Hold your baby.

It is magic.

Superpower #3

Emotional Security

This Superpower is inherently difficult to quantify. It takes more than 10,000 hours over many, many years of long, tedious, thankless patience before you realize any benefits.

But when you do see the benefits, they are huge.

The benefits are nearly beyond belief.

To be able to give your children a deeply-rooted sense of emotional security is more than a gift. It is more than gold or property. It is greater than happiness. It is deep and profound.

Giving your children emotional security is giving your children the ability to calmly and boldly walk into any situation.

It is a bigger and more powerful sense of self.

It is more important than money.

It is an understanding that your children will be able to make their own success in every environment –

no matter what comes.

It is an understanding that your children will be able to create their own happiness –

regardless of circumstance.

And they will be able to develop a secure foundation for their personality, their person, to grow on.

Build a new kind of human.

Build your kids into superheroes.

Hold your baby every day, all the time.

It is the most important thing you can do.

If you could, would you guide the lives of your children?

Knowing what you know now, would you want your kids to have the freedom to wander willy-nilly through life or focus, work hard and struggle?

Would you want your kids to have the ability to make the same mistakes that you have made?

Or do you think that making mistakes over and over again is a waste of time?

Would you want to help your kids make important decisions in life and take advantage of your experience?

Or do you think that it is more important to let them figure things out on their own?

LESSON FOUR

Grandma's magical secret

Years ago while my wife was pursuing her Ph.D., we lived in UCLA's married-student-housing. UCLA owns a bunch of real estate in West Los Angeles, houses, apartment buildings, commercial buildings, lots of different stuff. We lived in an old, 1950's, two-story, twelve unit apartment building about five miles southwest of UCLA. Our building was just one of a block of identical apartment buildings. UCLA used these buildings for married-student-housing.

There were twelve units in our building and another twelve units in the building across the courtyard. Each unit was rented (at super-cheap rates) to someone going to UCLA. Most of these were grad students. A little older, most with kids, sometimes the wife was the student, sometimes the husband, sometimes both. Each couple in our building was really very cool. There was an international feel to the place. Every other couple was from a different country: Italy, Israel, Poland, Columbia. It was a very cosmopolitan courtyard. In these 24 units, there were 16 or 20 little kids between zero and three. It was a blast.

There was an Olympic gymnast, an airline pilot, an international diamond dealer, a Polish grad student studying 18th Century Chinese literature written in English, a student preparing a paper on how a pattern of tied knots in rope represented an example of written language in pre-Columbian South America and another working on a Functional MRI study of what young college boys' brains look like while they were playing video games.

It was really fun to be there. Since we were all running on student time (no one worked 9-5), there was always somebody around. At any time of the day or night you could call down into the courtyard and say, "Hey, I'm going to Trader Joe's. Does anybody need anything?" or "We're out of Pampers; anyone got a spare?" or "I want to go for a run. Can someone watch my kid for a while?" And almost every Friday night someone would torch up the grill. With little planning, effort or invitation, we would have an impromptu dinner party with 20 couples and just as many kids.

It was really a heavenly place. Our own little village inhabited by super-smart, 20-something hipsters with kids.

Across the courtyard was a young woman from India. Her grandmother had come out to stay with her while she prepared for a wedding. Grandma was very charming. She was quiet and humble. She never wore Western clothing and was always dressed in brightly colored, traditional Indian gowns. She was my daughter's first babysitter. She would feed my daughter her favorite snack, tortillas, and catchup.

The grandmother had seven children. Each of her children was either a doctor or a lawyer. That was impressive. Raising seven healthy children is a huge achievement on its own, but raising seven kids so they all grow up to be successful doctors and lawyers is a completely different level of accomplishment.

It was extraordinary. It is even more impressive now that we have raised a couple kids of our own.

One day I asked Grandma, "How did you do it? How did you motivate seven kids to achieve so much?"

She said, "It was really very simple. There is a trick to it. Every time you pick up your child, you hold them tight, look deep into their eyes and say to them, 'You are going to be a doctor when you grow up.' You can say doctor or lawyer or whatever you want. You can say, 'You are going to help many, many people,' or 'You are going to walk on the moon,' or 'You are going to save the world.' You tell them what they are going to do. And you say it every day. Every time you hold them. Say the same thing every time and say it every time. You tell them that they are strong and you tell them that they are fearless. You tell them that they are smart and you tell them that they are beautiful."

I asked, "Wow, when do you start?"

"Right away, from the very first time you pick them up. But that is only one half of the strategy. The other important thing to know is that you have to remember when to stop. You say this every day until they are about three years old. Then you stop. Don't say it again. Just let their mind develop around that idea. You see, a child doesn't really record any memories until they are three or four. They don't remember anything in their conscious mind, but their unconscious mind remembers a lot. It remembers the feelings and emotions connected to where they were and what they were doing. You use this unconscious memory to try and guide them and mold them into the person that they might become. You talk to them and let them grow up around these ideas. Then you stop, and you let them grow up. Then when they get to be 12 or 13 years old, one day they will turn to you and say, 'You know, Mamma, I have had an idea. I think I want to be a doctor when I grow up.' It is all their idea. They come up with the motivation all on their own."

This idea went off like a bomb in my head. "Wow, does that really work?"

She said, "I tried it seven times and it worked seven times for me. I have seven beautiful children."

I thought about this idea a long time. I wondered if this would be a good thing to do for my kids. Part of me thought children need to be able to grow up in a free and open environment where they can make their own decisions. But then I thought that never really happens. Everyone is influenced by their environment, and the environment is never free from outside influence.

And then I thought a kid has to learn how to figure life out for himself. But then I thought, if I had known when I was younger what I know now, I would have started sooner and worked harder.

And then I thought trying to figure out what you want to be when you grow up is one of the most difficult decisions anyone ever has to make. And people are always asking high school kids, "What do you want to be when you grow up?" No seventeen-year-old kid knows the answer to that question. I know I didn't. But then I wondered, if I had the chance to make this decision easier if I could help my kids set a course sooner, would that be better?

And then I thought, if I would have been able to learn more from my dad, I might have been able to make fewer mistakes. If I could have learned from my dad's mistakes, I could have lived a better life. If I could learn from my dad's experience and my son could learn from my experience and his son could learn from my son's experience, think how much better my great-grandson's life will be.

So, if you could choose to guide your kid's life, would you? If you could decide before they were born what they wanted to be when they grew up, would you help them make that choice?

I wanted to see if this would work. I tried this with my kids. It worked with surprising results.

In the summer between her 5th and 6th year in school, my daughter seemed to wake up. It wasn't a flash of inspiration or an epiphany. It was more like a slow realization. She told me what she wanted to be when she grew up and she started to work. Even though it was summer and she didn't have the regiment of school, she started to work every day toward her goal.

She started to study seven days a week and she worked every day of the year. She was driven. Since that summer my daughter has studied every day. Even when the family was camping or on vacation, she would do some kind of project or be reading some book that was on her list of important books.

She worked on her birthday, on Christmas Day, Friday nights and weekends. She never takes a day off. She worked all the time. And she hasn't stopped. It is that kind of dedication and self-motivation that brings accomplishment. And that kind of step by step, brick by brick accomplishment that leads to success. And that kind of success that brings fulfillment.

Grandma's Little Magical Secret worked like a charm. I didn't have to hound my daughter. I didn't have to push her or pull her. I didn't have to threaten or demand. There was none of this, "You have to work harder, honey." Or, "Just try to do your best." All I had to do was get out of her way and clean up every once in a while. The motivation, her motivation, came from inside. She was and is self-motivated. She is motivated to push herself towards a goal.

So, if you could, would you guide the lives of your children? Would you do something now, something that seems so simple and easy, almost trivial, that could change their lives in a powerful and positive way?

Do you want to help your kids focus and work hard, especially during the intense high school years when it is most important?

Would you help your kids make important decisions years in advance that take advantage of your understanding and experience?

I tried Grandma's Little Secret on my kids and it worked in the most interesting and magical ways.

And I feel like this little secret is one of the most powerful tools that you can use to help your kids.

Superpower #4

Precognition

Precognition or "before acquiring knowledge" is an ability to see events in the future.

This Superpower gives you the ability to predict the future. But we are not really predicting the future. We are inventing it. Peter Drucker once said:

"The best way to predict the future is to invent it."

And, everyone would like to predict the future. The best way to do that is to create your own.

We want to invent a new world.

And we want that world to be bigger, brighter, and better than the world we live in now. We want this world to be freer, happier and more optimistic, a world in which everyone, every woman and every man has an opportunity to work their creative talents to their ultimate potential.

To do that we will need to raise a generation of superheroes.

You want to be able to build monster kids, people that can do anything, people that can envision, invent and create a new world, a better world.

If you can get your kids to work just one additional hour a day on something, just work one more hour a day on one thing, that time really builds up. It builds up like compound interest in the bank. It becomes an overwhelming mountain of understanding and mental momentum.

And this mental momentum takes a lot of effort.

And the best way to do this, the best way to insight, ignite and engage their motivation is to detonate their curiosity.

And the best way to do this is to invent and install these curiosity buttons before they even know what's going on.

If you have a very little baby or if you are about to have a baby, think about this idea; sit in a still, quiet space for a long time and think about what you will tell your baby.

Envision and invent the biggest and brightest future you can imagine.

And then pick a part in this future that your child will play.

Pick something and stick to it.

Think about it now and choose your thing.

Do you want them to be a doctor or a lawyer?

Do you want them to make a lot of money or become the President of the United States?

Do you want them to be a famous dancer or a brilliant musician?

Do you want them to live on Mars or explore the stars?

Do you want them to grow up to save the world?

Think about it. Pick something. And stick to it.

And whisper your vision softly in their ear every time you pick your baby up.

This Superpower is a magical little trick that will have a profound effect on the future of the world.

Is there a way you can light the spark of your child's mind?

At the beginning of life, a baby's brain is just a pile of tangled linguini of randomly firing neurons flashing and sparking and trying to start something.

What if there was a way to light the spark?

What if there was a way to start the fire?

What if you could trigger something that would bring order from the chaos?

And, get your baby's brain to blossom into a fully flaming mind?

LESSON FIVE

Listen to your baby

I clearly remember this one day when my daughter was just a baby, an infant, just a few months old. I was alone in the house with her. My wife had gone off to school and I was on Daddy Duty. It was early in the morning and she wasn't happy. She was crying - and crying - and crying. Nothing I could do would help. I didn't know how to be a dad and I didn't understand how to be a father. Was she mad? Was she sick? Was she hungry? Had she pooped her pants? Was she trying to poop but it wouldn't come out? Was she tired? Was she sleepy?

I felt completely helpless and a little bit scared. I didn't know what to do. I thought that there was some secret Mommy knowledge that I didn't have that would solve the problem, soothe her crying and save the day.

The first thing I did was to try everything. Like a guy fixing a car, I looked at the problem and tried to intuit some kind of solution. This is the strategy that my dad taught me. Ok, let's say you've got some kind of squeaking going on. You pop the hood and look around. Look to see if there is anything loose or wiggling or out of place. If that's not the case, look to see if you can figure out where the noise is coming from. Ok, it's coming from inside somewhere down, in and around the engine. Then you ask yourself, do you have anything else? Is it too hot or too cold? Have you tried to fix anything lately that you might have messed up? Is it getting enough gas? Does it have enough oil? Does it have enough water? Is it leaking anywhere? Is there anything else?

You take all of this information and you devise a plan. You say, "Ok, she's squeaking and she's hot, and there's water leaking out from somewhere. So what do we do?" We start by fixing or changing the easiest thing. The easiest thing to change is the V-belt. So we dig down in there and check the V-Belt. It is threadbare and worn out, so let's change that. We start taking things apart, we get closer to the problem, we change the V-belt and we try it again. Hmmm, still more squeaking—that wasn't it.

What else could it be? As we get closer to the problem, we see that it's leaking right down near the front of the engine, so we wiggle the water pump pulley to see if it's loose. We continue with this iteration until we find the problem. We may end up fixing three or four things that weren't the problem before we actually stumble onto the right solution, but we keep trying until we get the problem solved.

So, this is what I would do for my baby. I would change her and feed her and burp her. Was she too hot? I'll take her jammies off. Was she too cold? I'll wrap her in a blanket. I would try one thing at a time until I stumbled upon the solution to the problem.

The whole time I would be listening to her and trying to figure it out. After a couple years, you get pretty good at figuring out what the problems are. Just like my dad and cars. After an engineering degree and thousands of hours working on cars, my dad's mechanical intuition was very acute. My dad is a car whisperer. If I was broken down 2000 miles from home, he could sense the source of the squeak from the way I mimicked the sound over the phone. He could diagnose the car problem and devise the quickest fix with just the sounds of me squeaking and grunting into a payphone in the back of a noisy bar. He was amazing.

Like my dad's intuitions about car problems, I've gained intuitions about baby problems. I can tell what is wrong with a baby by the sound of its cry. I can tell from a baby's cry if she is hungry or cold, tired or frightened, sick or just needs to poop. I am a baby whisperer. And with a little practice, you can learn to be a baby whisperer too.

But you have to listen. You have to learn how to listen to your baby. You have to actively listen to your baby and learn to connect the kind of cry with the kind of problem that you discover.

And this is important. Listen to him or her. They are trying to tell you what the problem is. They are trying to talk to you. So listen to your baby. Hold them close, look into their eyes, talk to them slowly and clearly and ask them what the problem is.

There is more to this than just trying to find a way to help your baby stop crying.

It's time to level up –

It's not just that listening to your baby helps you solve the problem.

It is a much bigger deal than that. Listening to your baby lets her know that you are listening. Once they know you're listening, their brain opens up. That first time your baby realizes that you are listening and that there is a positive feedback, the concept of communication explodes in their brain. It's like a flower blooming or a bulb popping for the first time. Your baby realizes that talking is a thing. They learn that they can "talk" to you and that communicating can provide positive feedback.

This happens very early on, right away; it might start on their first day. And it's a big deal. Look for it. Encourage it. Enable it. It will make a huge difference in the way your child's mind develops.

I believe that the neural superstructure for human communication is hardwired into every human's brain. The basic architecture is there. But it needs to be developed. It needs to be exercised. The sooner you can trigger this positive feedback, the stronger the mental muscles will grow. And if you start early and work, these communication muscles when they are very young will develop into a kind of superhuman communication skill. If you develop these skills early, your babies will find the skill of learning quickly and they will develop the skill of learning from abstract. This is a super important skill.

Most animals learn from firsthand experience. They see something steaming over a fire, they reach out and touch it and they get burned. This pain teaches them a lesson. The lesson is that they should not touch things steaming over the fire.

A human, on the other hand, can learn by abstract. They can have another human tell them not to touch things on the fire. They can hear an explanation of an abstract idea and learn in advance of an experience what to do in a situation that they have never encountered. This is learning by abstract. This is a uniquely human trait. And you want to develop this trait in your children as quickly as you can.

Once your baby realizes that their actions produce reactions from you, they will begin to learn that communication is a thing. Once they learn that communication is a thing, they will begin to shape their actions to elicit a specific positive reaction from you. As this happens, their brain will begin to rewire itself and the neural networks associated with communication will begin to blossom and grow stronger.

From there they will need to go through several steps: from shaped action/reaction to mimicked action to miming to oral identification of objects (pointing and naming) to abstract concepts. This will take some time, so you want to get started as soon as you can.

Once your children learn how to learn from abstract concepts, their learning accelerates. And the sooner you can engage this process, the faster a kind of multiplying effect happens. The neural superstructures in their brain develop early and grow stronger. And the stronger these neural structures grow, the faster they will be able to learn from abstract.

There is a way you can light the spark of your child's mind.

There is a way to start the fire.

It is time to trigger an organized mind and bring order from the chaos.

Get your baby's brain to blossom into a fully flaming human mind.

Listen to your baby.

Abstract Learning

Learning from abstract is a Superpower, and enabling your children to learn this way will give them a superhuman learning skill.

Just like any part of your body, the more you use something, the stronger it gets. The longer you ride your bike, the harder your ass gets. The more curls you do, the bigger your biceps get, and if you grow up playing tennis, it is kind of creepy how your right wrist is just bigger than your left.

It is the same thing with your brain. The more you think about something, the stronger that portion of your brain becomes. If you think about music and learn to play an instrument, your brain will build entirely new neural networks in your head to accommodate this new need. If you learn to play soccer, your body will reinforce the myelin sheaths covering the dendrites of the nerves that control your feet. And if you decide to pursue an engineering degree, you will discover at the end of your four years of study you can do ridiculously complicated algebraic equations in your head.

It is important to keep this concept in your mind while talking to an infant. Everything you say and everything you do will change the way your baby's brain develops. So you want to start communicating with your baby as quickly as you can. Look at them while you're talking to them, and touch their hands and move their feet. Play little games like hide and seek. Hold your kid's feet while they are sitting in a bouncy chair and move them in circles like they are running or riding a bike.

It is also important to keep in mind that these specific actions enforce specific parts of the brain. The larger structures of the mind are also in play. Think about it like freeways versus highways versus neighborhood streets. There are larger structures in your brain that control and direct pre-thought or sub-thought. These are structures that build ideas like grammar and sentence or paragraph structure.

When you get your baby to start to understand that bilateral communication is a thing, her brain will start to develop and reinforce the freeways and highways inside her mind that control the logic and reason of grammar and linguistic thought.

And this is a very big deal.

Talking to your baby and communicating with your baby in an empathetic, creature-to-creature way starts an electrical fire in the tangled linguini of her mind.

React to his or her actions and let them know that they will get positive feedback from you. Carry your baby around and talk to them, telling them what you are doing. Give him or her the play by play, like a sports commentator, naming the utensils and ingredients of your Monday night's marinara.

Everything you do and everything you say, every moment you spend with your baby will build their brain bigger and stronger.

And teaching your children to communicate early will reinforce the freeways and highways of logical reason and thought. These neural networks are the foundation of abstract thought. And the stronger these networks become, the more connections they make, the better their processes will be.

Teach your children how to learn from concepts and their ability to learn will accelerate.

Learning from abstract is a Superpower, and enabling your children to learn this way will give them a superhuman learning skill.

Let's talk about the opposite of that.

Let's say you, for some reason, decide not to listen to your baby, or maybe even worse—ignore your baby.

There are three levels to this. For the sake of illustration, let's invent three hypothetical babies and three hypothetical dads. We'll call them Stupid Daddy, Bad Daddy, and Evil Daddy.

Stupid Daddy, Bad Daddy and Evil Daddy all have the same problem. They each have the task of taking care of a little baby. Taking care of a baby is very hard work. No one really tells you what to do or how to do it. Most people just have to make it up as they go along. Some lucky people can call their moms or someone else that has done it before. Some people read books about how to raise a kid. Some people have support groups, like other mommies and daddies, that they can call for guidance. But I'll bet most of the folks raising kids today have nothing. They have no idea what they're doing and they just have to wing it. I was one of the lucky dads. I had all three. I had my moms (my mom and my mom-in-law) that I could call. I had all kinds of books to read and I had a large support group—a lot of friendly neighbors that I could talk too.

Another reason that it's hard is that it takes your complete concentration. If you want to do it right, you have to take yourself down to the same level as your child. Babies are simple creatures. A one-month-old baby probably has the same mental capacity as a rabbit. It's not really thinking yet. It's just taking it all in and recording everything. At this point the baby is mostly adjusting its eyes, its ears, its smell and its connection to its body, using its biofeedback loops to line everything up.

If you want to hold the attention of the baby, you can't do it from your own mental state. It doesn't work that way. To relate to a baby or a small child, you have to slow your mind down and simplify your thoughts until you are thinking at the same level as the baby.

This is very hard to do. It takes a lot of energy and it is very frustrating. I mean, you could be thinking about what you were wanting to think about. You could be reading a book or watching TV. But noooo, you have to be thinking at the level of a rabbit, almost nothing, to get yourself down to the level of the baby just to try and start to take care of it.

It takes a lot of effort and a lot of work. It is kind of like a very high level of Zen meditation.

Since it is so hard to do and takes a lot of energy, most people don't want to do it. It's just too hard.

So let's say that Stupid Daddy, Bad Daddy, and Evil Daddy are taking care of their babies. Each one is alone and each one doesn't know what they're doing and each one doesn't have anyone to call. The baby starts crying and they don't know what to do.

Let's take these examples one at a time.

First, we'll talk about Stupid Daddy. Stupid Daddy tries to solve the problem the best he knows how. He will jiggle some keys, turn the TV on or give her an iPad to try and distract her. He is not really listening to his baby and he is not trying to relate to his baby on an intuitive, empathetic level. In the end, Stupid Daddy will leave her in a room with the TV on and hope that she stops crying and falls asleep. Stupid Daddy isn't bad; he just doesn't know what to do and doesn't have any help. Stupid Daddy's daughter might not get her diaper changed until Mommy gets home from work.

Next, let's think about Bad Daddy—same situation, same scenario. Bad Daddy's baby starts to cry and Bad Daddy isn't having any of it. He thinks this is a huge waste of his time. Bad Daddy straps his daughter in a high chair so that she can't hurt herself or get away; then he sneaks out the back door and heads over to his friend's to play video games. Four hours later, Bad Daddy sneaks in the back door and finds his daughter asleep in the highchair.

Now let's look at Evil Daddy. Evil Daddy was raised by a 16-year-old single mom that dropped out of school when she found out she was pregnant. Evil Daddy has no idea what to do. It's 10 am and his daughter starts crying. Evil Daddy may have had a couple beers for breakfast and just wants to get out of his place and hook up with his friends. Evil Dad's daughter is crying and it is starting to piss him off. He talks to her and tells her to be quiet. She feels the stress and cries even harder. He screams at her to shut up. That action and volume scares her and she has a meltdown. He screams at her again. When she cries louder, Evil Daddy slaps her across the face. She screams even more, and he leaves the room, leaves the house and leaves his baby crying.

Here is what's going on from the baby's point of view. With each of these situations, the baby is in a negative feedback loop. It's kind of like the tit-for-tat economic strategy. The tit-for-tat economic strategy goes something like this. Two businessmen form an alliance. At the beginning of the alliance, they just have to trust each other. You tell me what you are going to do and I will trust you. If it works out and you end up doing what you say you're going to do, then businessman A pays businessman B and the relationship moves forward. But if businessman B cheats businessman A, then the strategy changes and businessman A should respond by cheating businessman B.

Another way of saying this is: You play nice with strangers on your first encounter. If the stranger plays nice in response, then you continue to play nice. This is a positive feedback loop. If, on the other hand, the stranger cheats you, your response should be to go on defense or cheat him back— a tit for a tat. This is a negative feedback loop. This is the most successful long-term gaming strategy. You either have a win-win scenario or you have a win-lose scenario.

In our scenario, the baby will try to reach out. The baby is vulnerable and presents a submissive posture. If the baby receives attention and caring, a positive feedback, the baby will be at ease, relaxed and secure. But if the baby receives no response, the baby is on edge. The creature is insecure and confused. The baby feels that this strategy is not working and it pulls back and is guarded. The baby intuits that the initial strategy is unsuccessful and it must change to the win-lose strategy, go on defense and protect itself.

In the Evil Daddy situation, it is even worse. In a violent situation, the baby understands that there is no reason to allow itself to be vulnerable at any time. There is no reason to reach out or try to interact with other people. Once the baby learns that interaction brings pain, the baby shuts down and goes on defense. Raised in a violent environment, the baby's brain is automatically rewired. Large portions of the child's brain are permanently dedicated to defense and aggression. This is why children raised in a violent environment tend to exhibit psychopathic behavior as adults.

The neglect and abuse of very young children will severely impact their cognitive development. When a baby is abused and the baby switches to a win-lose, defensive mind strategy, the mind of the child literally rewires itself. Whole sections of the mind are permanently rewired and rededicated to defense. These sections of the mind are no longer available to higher level, empathetic cognition. This is how a psychopath is made. Within a neglectful or abusive environment, the mind develops completely differently. It is a mind without empathy and without the higher level cognitive abilities of a cared-for, loved child.

Under the direction of a loving, caring parent, the child's mind can grow and develop in a different way. If a child is raised in a secure environment, entire portions of their mind will open up. The mind will blossom. Their mind will be able to develop higher level thinking. Instead of dedicating these sections of the mind to defensive and aggressive behaviors, these sections can now be used for culture, creativity, and empathy.

If you want to raise an empathetic child, a child with the ability to reach its full human potential, you must learn to commune with your child on his or her level in a loving, secure environment. You need to be able to clear your mind and empathize with your child on their level. It is really hard to do and takes a lot of energy, but it is well worth the time and effort.

This is why it is so important to hold your baby every day. As that homeless Obi-Wan Kenobi on the bus told me, love your baby.

"All's you have to do is love them. I mean really love them. I mean deep down. You have to love them. You have to let them know that they are loved. You have to hold them every chance you get because you might not get another chance. You have to squeeze them tight and keep them safe."

How do you encourage feedback?

How do you spark curiosity and focus attention?

How do you inspire your kids to learn and communicate?

LESSON SIX

Talk to your baby

My typical day at the UCLA married-student-housing went something like this.

My wife and I would wake up early and sneak out of bed. We would leave our daughter to sleep as long as we could. We would get up and make coffee. My wife would eat something and get ready for school. I would usually hang out, distract the baby and do whatever I could to help my wife out the door. Sometimes she would take the bus, sometimes she would drive, and sometimes we would drive her up to school and drop her off in our ratty, old, desert sand Volvo station wagon.

My wife was in the final phases of her program at UCLA. She was very intense. It was not unusual for her to be up and out of the house by 7:00 and not back home till midnight.

I would usually spend the mornings playing with my daughter. Sometimes we would go for a jog in her jogging stroller. Sometimes we would go for a bike ride. Sometimes she would play with the other kids in our building. Sometimes we would hook up with another daddy/daughter combo and walk up to Starbucks for a kid's hot cocoa.

What I was trying to do was tucker her out. I was trying to get her tired so that she would take a nap. We would get home from whatever adventure we had going, I would feed her a bottle of wonderful frozen mommy's goodness, and then we would go into the bedroom and lay down. Most times she would fight. She didn't like taking naps and she would always put on a big fuss going down for her mid-afternoon nap.

I would lie on my back holding her on my chest. She would wiggle and squawk and I would hold her tight. After a while, we would both fall asleep. After a quick power nap, I would wake up and slowly and carefully slide her off my chest and on to the bed. Then I would sneak out of the room and get back to work.

This was my magical time. This is when I got most of my work done. I was starting a business, so I had a lot to do. I was working on a patent, filing articles of incorporation, designing parts, building prototypes, sourcing material, and all kinds of business stuff. Most of what I did I could do in my jammies in our apartment with a baby in one hand and a mug of coffee in the other. And most of my work I got done in little gaps between being a dad.

One day when my daughter was about—hmmm, let me think... she couldn't walk yet, so she had to be less than one. My daughter was in the bedroom taking a nap and I was writing something on our computer. I was on a tight deadline. I had to get this one thing done and I had to get it done today. I was furiously pounding away at the keyboard when my happy baby daughter came crawling around the corner and out of the bedroom.

I was like, not yet, not now. I need ten more minutes. Give me ten more minutes, please. If I could only get ten more minutes, I could get this thing done, click send and get it off to my partners in China.

But no, my daughter wouldn't have any of it.

She came crawling out of the bedroom and wanted to play. She crawled over to my chair and pulled herself up next to me. I ignored her for as long as I could. I would turn to her and say, "Please, oh please, could I have another ten minutes?" She would look at me and squawk, "You have to play with me now," in some kind of proto baby language.

Long before our kids were even conceived, my wife and I had made plans on how we wanted to raise them. One of those plans was how we were going to talk to them and teach them. We had made a conscious effort to think about how we were going to teach our kids. And part of that plan was how we were going to talk to our babies.

When you talk to your babies in adult language, with long, multisyllabic words and complicated sentence structure, your baby has to start, from the very beginning, untangling your language. This is a very good puzzle for a young mind to ponder. It takes more time and more effort for your child to struggle with your language, but it is very good for them. When you talk to your child like an adult, they grow up using the same cadence and sentence structure that they heard as a baby. They grow up hearing and learning long and complicated words. And they start from the very beginning using adult words and complicated sentence structure.

We had made a conscious effort to talk to our baby daughter like an adult and now was no different.

I looked down at her and in my best low, manly daddy voice said, "Excuse me, but I can't play with you now. I have work to do. Go over there to the bookshelf and read a book. I will come over there in a little while and read with you."

Now granted she was a baby. I knew she was a baby. She couldn't walk. She couldn't talk. She couldn't read. I was sure that she didn't even know what a book was.

Anyway, she sat back down and crawled away. I turned back to the task at hand and concentrated on my deadline. I was almost done—just a few more points.

A couple minutes later I felt a tug on my pants. I looked down and gasped in shock. There was my daughter pulling herself up to my level with a copy of Good Night Gorilla in her hand. I couldn't believe it. She had heard what I said, crawled over to the bookshelf, picked out her favorite book and brought it over for me to read to her. She what? This can't be real.

I couldn't believe it. She knew what I was saying. She knew what I was talking about. She knew what a book was. She knew what reading was. Before she could walk, before she was coordinated enough to make simple sounds with her mouth, she understood words and sentences and thoughts and language. This meant that she had been listening to us the whole time. My wife and I had thought that we were just

71

talking to each other or talking to ourselves, but NO. Our daughter had been listening.

The shear monumental weight of the moment took hold of me.

I forgot about what I was doing and grabbed my daughter, lifted her towards the sky like Mufasa and said, "You have awoken!"

I immediately called my wife and told her the story. Our baby was awake; she was a little person now. I was blown away.

Here's the thing.

The important lesson to learn here is to talk to your baby.

I have been thinking about thinking most of my life. I have been wondering about consciousness since I was in high school. I had been asking questions like: "What is the mind?" "How do we think?" "What is our consciousness, how does it develop and how does it work?" I had been watching my daughter for signs of awareness or awakening and here it was. Here was the moment I had been waiting for. I had put down a baby, an amoeba, a thing with the mind of a rabbit, for a nap and two hours later a little girl had woken up and come out into the world. It blew me away. I was in awe.

It is important to listen to your baby and watch for the way she develops. Talk to your baby all the time assuming that she can hear you and understands what you are saying. Watch what she is doing and react to her actions so that she feels the connection and understands that she gets feedback. Talk to your baby like an adult, with big words and complicated sentence structure. The baby begins to encode the cadence and rhythm of your communication from the very first time you talk to her. She will grow up talking the way she was talked to as a baby and as a child.

Watch what she is doing and listen. Talk to your baby and listen to what she is trying to tell you.

This awakening happens much faster than anyone ever expects. Understand that they are going to be listening to you from the moment they are born. Assume that their minds will blossom early. Watch for this awakening and celebrate it when it happens. With you in her feedback loop, your baby will develop much, much faster.

You have to encourage feedback. You must engage with your baby and talk to her. Your actions will spark her curiosity and focus her attention. When you talk to your baby, you inspire them to learn and communicate.

Talk to your baby.

Superpower #6

Schema

What is human consciousness? Was that what I was looking at? Was I witnessing the dawn of my daughter's consciousness?

I'm not sure. Maybe. In a way, I think I was watching my daughter's cognitive awakening in that brief and crazy moment.

So what is consciousness? And how does it work?

I have an idea about how my mind works.

I call this idea your Schema. Other people have had similar ideas. Scott Adams has an idea he calls Filter. Scott thinks that you should proactively program your mind to work in a certain way. He says that the best thing to do is to design your Filter so that it A) makes you happy and B) enables you to predict the future. I think that this is a good idea.

I would like to present my version of this idea. I will start by defining terms.

I define the word Schema here as a model of reality that your mind builds in your head. In this piece, I will use the words Filter and Schema interchangeably. Here is how I think my mind works.

Everyone in the world, every man, woman, and child, every creature for that matter, wanders around the planet collecting information. Its eyes learn to focus, its ears learn to hear, and its body and mind senses and records everything they hear, see, taste and touch as it moves through the world. Your mind takes in all this information, and as it is recording it splits the information into quantified chunks, like pictures, like flashes of discreet time.

A flash is an incident, a brief moment of time in which something happens to you.

For this example, I am going to break down one flash of time according to the sensor suite that has collected the information. You have your eyes that record the visual images, your ears that record the sounds, your body that records your physical location, including your position, orientation, rotation, and direction as well as the first and second derivatives of each of these inputs. On top of all of this, your mind also records many layers of time and place. It records the time not in time as we know it in minutes and seconds but in biological time in chunks of changes or flashes of incidences.

Your mind also builds context into these flashes like your place in your family, your place within generations, your place in your neighborhood, your place within your community, your state, your nation, your place on the Earth, your place in the solar system and your place in the universe.

All these inputs are filed using the mental, linguistic, religious and social systems that you were born into and taught as a child. For instance, if you were raised speaking German, each object that you know was connected to a German word and those words were built into sentences and paragraphs, and these paragraphs have a very specific structure and logic that is very, very different from, say, Chinese or Russian. And this language structure provides a scaffolding or a filing system that becomes hard-wired into your brain as you grow from infant to adult. If you think about it, you can imagine dozens or hundreds or maybe even millions of different logic filing systems that are built into every human's head. There is the language structure, the religious structure, the family structure, the culture structure and other things that are multi-layered, intertwined, and tangled up inside your mind that your mind uses to collect, tag, compress and record each flash of time that your mind records.

Each individual has their own eyes. Each individual has their own set of ears. Each individual has their own pair of opposing thumbs, and each individual has their own set of logic scaffoldings that they use to collect, tag, time-stamp, compress and record each flash of time that they move through.

On top of that, there is another layer of critical contextual connection. As your mind records this data, it builds many, many millions or billions of contextual connections between each of the data flows, between each of the sensor suites that are collecting data. And as my mind does this, it is constantly updating all of the other memories that are touching and associated with this moment.

To explain this idea a little further, I am going to take just one flash of time and one sensor suite and try to detangle the contextual connection of just the one very smallest piece of data. I am going to try and place the color brown.

As I look across the room, I see the other wall of my living room. On that wall is an old picture of a train moving through Montana. Around that picture is a picture frame. The picture frame is brown. If I were to try to rewind the recording of the flash of time and analyze what contextual connections my mind may have made while I quickly looked across the room, it may have been something like this.

My mind knows the time, day, date, and season of when that flash occurred. This time is not recorded in numbers like a clock. The time stamp is recorded against my biological clock. This clock might "tick" or count the number of flashes of my consciousness. This clock began counting the number of flashes or incidents of my consciousness from the moment I was born. The clock keeps track of the moments that I am conscious regardless of whether I am asleep or awake. Each of my sensor suite data flows—my eyes, ears, nose, body position, etc.—are time-stamped as they come into my head. Each of these chunks of data might hit my head at different times. For instance, light travels faster than sound, so the visual images hit my head before the sound hits my ears. To compensate for this latency problem, my mind or my clock has to somehow adjust the time stamps of the different data flows so that the incident reports align. So it might go something like this.

I accidentally touch a hot pan on the stove. First, my eyes see that I touch the pan. Next my ears hear a sizzle of my skin burning, and finally, the sense of pain makes its way up my nerves to my head. My mind must hold each of these different data flows in some kind of buffer until the slowest incident sequential data point, my nerve pain, comes into my head. Only then is the incident or flash time-stamped, ensuring that my mind connects all of the inputs to one specific event.

So each flash is somehow time stamped.

Your mind also knows the temperature and the weather outside. It also knows your position in the room, the position, direction, rotational position, and all the other nine different dimensional measurements that describe my place in this space. I know the position of the sun in the sky, the position of this house on the street, the position of the street in the neighborhood. I know the position of my body in this chair and the position of the chair in the room. I know the distance to that wall—not distance in numbers, mind you, but the distance in biological space. I know that that thing on the wall is a picture. I know the picture is covered in glass. I know the glass is held by a frame. I know the frame is made out of wood. I know the frame is made of straight, vertical and horizontal lines. I know the frame is brown. I know the exact shade of brown out of thousands of other shades of brown and how that color and shade will change according to the light in the room, the time of day, the month of the year and the weather outside.

As my mind subconsciously collects, time stamps, compresses and contextualizes this flash, the wetware/software creation that is my mind reaches back into and through the mental scaffoldings in my head to connect this specific shade of brown to every single instance of flash of memory where I might have seen this specific shade of brown. In this context, my Schema automatically guesses that this brown is probably wood and might be mahogany. This brown is part of a frame that holds a picture but not a mirror or a window. And this brown is on the wall in my living room and has been part of my environment for many years.

On top of that, I have all of the historical spatial information that my mind has collected over the last four years about this room, my place in it, the stuff in the room and how that stuff is organized.

On top of that, I have the many hundreds of linguistic references connected with brown, picture, frame, wall, train and all of the rest of that.

On top of that, I have all of the cultural scaffolding connected to the picture and house and home frame and brown that allows me to place the idea of a picture on a wall in a house on my street in this neighborhood etc., etc.

Other information that is probably included in this time-stamped flash is the general news of the day. What is happening in my life. Where my kids are and what they are doing. Where my wife is and what time she will get home this evening. Who the President of the United States is and what the stock market is up to. And more importantly, I am recording why I am writing this, what I am thinking and where this specific thought fits into the rest of my argument.

And the contextual connections go on and on and down and down into millions and billions of connections that build context to this color brown on this picture frame around this picture hanging on the wall across the room from me now.

I can't even begin to know all the different ways my mind builds context. But that is what it does. That is how it works and that is what it is made for.

But –

That is not my point.

My point is, under that, inside of that, looking at that tangled web of interconnected scaffoldings, you can see the reason for the mind. The mind builds this system of collection, tagging, categorization, compression, and storage of flashes of time so that it can build something else. It needs to build a device, a special kind of simulator. It builds this simulator so that it can have not the memories and not even a way to recall the memories; it builds the device so that it can have the device. It is the device that your mind is after. It is the device, this simulator, that Darwinian evolution has created. And it is the device, this massive multi-parallel system of contextualizing scaffoldings, that is the valuable component of this creation.

It is this device that I call Schema. It is the device that Scott Adams calls Filter.

So here is what you do with the device.

This device, this software suite, this simulator, is sitting in your subconscious. You can't see it. You don't have access to it. It is inside your head, underneath your conscious mind. This device is like a virtual copy of the universe. It is like a hallucination of reality. It is like a parallel, virtual world that your mind has made to run simulations in.

What you do and what everyone else does is take this device and as new information comes at you, you quickly test this new information by filtering it through your Schema. Your mind runs a very quick simulation and uses this information to try to predict the future.

Your mind collects the new information, feeds it into your Schema and tries to run a simulation in your mind before events in the real world play out. It is like you are a guy in left field that sees the player swing and hears the crack of the bat and sees the ball fly and tries to predict where the ball is going to land so that he can get there first and catch it.

The ball player uses his Schema, his internal virtual reality hallucination, to predict the path of the ball, and he uses this prediction to change the future. If his predictions are correct, he will be able to catch the ball and change the future. If his predictions are off by even one small degree or microsecond of time, he will miss the catch, a runner will score and the other team will win the game. If he catches the ball, the future will change again, and his destiny and the destiny of his team will change again and move in a different direction.

So, it is my conjecture that the man with the better Schema—a Schema that is closer to base reality, a Schema that is more correct and more precise—will be able to predict the future more correctly more often. And if you can build your Schema to be more realistic, more precise, you will be able to become more successful because you predict the future better more often.

If you ever want to build a true human intelligence AI, the first thing you have to do is build a massively multi-paralleled, multi-scaffolding machine that collects, deconstructs, tags, time-stamps, compresses, and records each flash of information that contextualizes and cross-references all of the information in the world.

But is that all there is? Is that what human consciousness is? I don't know, maybe. Maybe that's all there is. Maybe our minds have evolved in a way just to build scaffolding modules, and they just layer these modules up next to each other and on top of each other over and over and over again. And maybe human consciousness just emerges out of the architecture of that layering.

I'm not sure if there is a bright defining line or moment between being conscious and not being conscious. I mean for sure human consciousness is something different than, say, the consciousness of a dog or a lobster or a plant or a Roomba, but is human consciousness something that just flips on like a switch? And was I witnessing that magical moment when my daughter's light was turned on?

I think so. I thought so then and my mind has not changed. I put my daughter down for a nap and two hours later she woke up different. It was just like that. Blink! She's on.

But I'm not sure that consciousness comes on like that. I think it comes on more like a dimmer switch. I think it clicks on and then slowly ramps up and gets brighter and brighter.

For instance, I feel like I am a lot more conscious now at 60 than I was at 50. And at 50 I felt a lot more conscious than I felt at 40. At 40 I felt a lot more conscious than I felt at 30. And so on and so on. I think my conscious grows and gets deeper and deeper the older I get.

So maybe what I was seeing when I looked down to realize that my daughter had understood a sentence, my thought, a flash, was just the very first flicker of human consciousness clicking on.

And this is what you are looking for in your kids.

Look for it. Encourage it.

Try to help your children proactively program their mind and develop their Schema to be true and correct. Work on your Schema at the same time and try to find ways to build your consciousness as close to base reality as you possibly can. Look for and discover or invent logic systems, mental scaffoldings, in language, religions, families, cultures and in every realm of human life that help you predict the future quicker and more correctly.

And then teach your kids these systems.

If you can help your children build a Schema that is more precise, more correct, they will be able to predict the future quicker and more correctly.

If they possess a simulator that can closely predict the future, they will be able to make better decisions. Decisions that are more correct more of the time.

And this will enable them to have a more successful life.

Being able to correctly predict the future is having a Superpower. And building a Schema that is better aligned with base reality will enable your kids to predict the future better than anyone else.

The closer to base reality your child's Schema becomes, the more successful, more fulfilled and happier your child will be.

Section 2

WHY DO THIS?

Why have kids?

I mean, you only have one life. Right?
You may have heard the saying YOLO.
You only live once—Carpe Diem, seize the day.
Looking at this one way, the saying tells you to take big risks, live life with gusto, grab life by the balls, live for the Now and enjoy an exciting life.
But the long-term implications of this saying are quite dark. The saying infers that life, in general, has no purpose or meaning and that your life specifically is insignificant and has no value. The saying infers that you might as well not waste any time making long-term goals or trying to do anything to make the world a better place.
This saying is trying to tell us that our highest purpose in life is to chase after meaningless diversion.
Live for the moment. There is no tomorrow.
I don't believe that. And my beliefs are from real life lessons I've learned and not from what I read in a book or heard in a song.
After high school, I spent ten years as a ski bum. I lived the highest form of the hedonistic life. Inspired by POWDER Magazine, I moved to Aspen and lived off my wits.
It seemed to me that the mega-rich and the ultra-successful worked really hard and put in the long hours so that they could fly into Aspen on the weekends to drink champagne, snort cocaine and dine on strawberries and whipped cream. To me, I figured that if I played my cards right, I could skip all of that hard work and all of those long hours and just thrash around in cocaine and whipped cream.
And I did.
It turned out to be very easy. It was very easy for me to live the life of a billionaire by just hanging out with billionaires. You figure out what they like to do and go hang out where they like to go. For me, it was sailing and skiing.
As it turns out, most billionaires spend most of their time working hard on making a successful life, so they don't really

know how to ski very well. And they like to hang out with kids that do. They like to hang out with the locals that know the cool places to go. They like to hang out with the people that like to take risks and party. And it was easy for me to give them what they wanted.

So I lived as a hardcore heathen for a decade, wallowing in the sex and drugs and Rock and Roll, as much as I wanted, all of the time.

But then a funny thing happened. I realized that it was boring.

I learned, from firsthand experience, that the party isn't the goal for successful people. The party isn't the objective. The celebration is not the purpose.

Partying your brains out without something to celebrate is empty and meaningless. It is the hard work that is fulfilling. The party is just a recognition of success. If you throw a celebration without the pain, frustration, and exhaustion of actually working towards a goal and accomplishing a hard-fought task, you are just wallowing in a mirage.

And that is what I was doing for those ten years. I was gliding oiled and naked through a hallucination.

Because really that's what I thought I was supposed to do. That's what the media was telling me life was all about.

Live for the moment—life has no meaning, so why not just party?

I was eating the cake before the party. I was joining the celebration before the games had begun. And I learned that it was empty and boring.

And I feel like that is the main message in the media now.

Don't waste your youth working hard or raising children. It is a lot more fun to wallow around in hedonistic diversion.

So why do this? Why do something so difficult and time-consuming as raising kids when you can be off somewhere exciting in an orgasmic rush, partying your brains out in a ski resort?

Well, I'm going to start here with three simple stories from very good friends of mine that molded the way I think about family. I have changed their names to protect their privacy.

Matthew

Matt is a spiritual man. He is the hardest working guy I know, and he is very serious. He is humble and strong in a way that lets you know that his humility comes from his strength. I am lucky enough to be able to spend some of Matt's time, for his time is very valuable.

Matt makes sure that he spends time every week directly caring for others. Whether that time is spent at his church, counseling inmates at the local prison, or donating energies to a charitable cause, Matt puts in the time.

As part of this effort, one time Matt accepted the burden of assisting with a local hospice. He would meet each week with old men nearing the ends of their lives. He would just sit with them and visit. Some of these guys were your average guys, and some of these guys were important, powerful, wealthy men. Matt's contribution was to meet with one of these men each week for an hour or two while they moved through hospice.

Matt wouldn't tell me about any direct interactions with the men, for that was given in confidence. But Matt did tell me about the lessons they learned—what those men valued and how they set their priorities.

Matt told me that while he sat with these men near the end of their lives and talked, one strong theme seemed to come up over and over again.

They all wished that they had spent more time with their family. They had all told Matt that making money was great, buying big real estate and using their power was a lot of fun, doing great things and achieving high ranks of status was exciting, but the one thing that they wish they would have done was to have spent more time with their kids. In the end, they had recognized that the most valuable thing that any man could have was a strong, happy and healthy family. The relationships that they had had with their children were more valuable than all the money that they had ever made.

These are guys that could buy pretty much anything they wanted. These are guys that worked hard their whole lives and amassed enough power to have things done the way they wanted. And what did they want? They wanted stronger families. They wanted to have better relations with their kids.

Mark

Being a ski bum, you get to meet dozens and dozens of new people every year. Every October a new crop of ski bums show up in ski towns around the world. Towns like Aspen and Verbier, Jackson Hole or Argentiere. Most of these kids are lost souls, someone that can't sit still, someone that questions reality. The kind of kid that is unsatisfied with the idea of having their circumstance dictate their destiny.

These people need to act. They need to force life's moments. They need to push themselves into exciting circumstances. These are the kinds of souls that end up in ski resorts for a season. Some of these kids come from nothing and nowhere, and some of these kids are the castaways of the richest people in the world.

One of these guys was my good friend Mark. Mark and I were crew on a racing yacht moored in Honolulu. Mark was a bright, fun, humble, healthy guy that was taking some time off from school to sort things out. I didn't know it at first, but after living with the guy for three months, I realized that Mark was part of a very wealthy family. His family had a privately held business that had been in the family for five generations, passing the business down from father to son for almost 100 years.

Mark's family owned the multimillion-dollar racing yacht that I was working on.

This family was not only successful financially but successful as a family. It is hard enough to grow a business for more than a couple generations, but it is nearly impossible to raise children in opulence and have the children maintain their sanity and become successful in their own right.

I got to know Mark, and I got to watch how Mark interacted with his father. What I saw was shocking. It was nothing like the strange and twisted impressions that you pick up from watching TV shows like Dallas or reading stories like the Great Gatsby.

The thing that blew me away was their values. While living on the boat I got to see the way that Mark's dad valued his son. Mark would tell me stories of how, while growing up, his dad would take him on an adventure almost every weekend. Every weekend they would go out camping or hunting or fishing or just riding horses.

Here was a man that commanded a huge multi-national corporation. Here was a man that could afford to sail a multimillion-dollar racing yacht in open ocean races across the globe. Here was a man that had a fleet of private jets to take him anywhere he wanted to go. And where did he want to go? He wanted to go camping with his son almost every weekend. This series of actions demonstrated how much the father valued the son. I believe that what you spend time doing is what you end up loving and that love is an action. When you examine the time and effort that Mark's father invested in his son, it is easy to see how much the father loved the son.

And it showed. Mark was one of the most confident, secure and strong guys I had ever met. He had a commanding presence. The way he moved, the way he walked, the way he talked was impressive. He was always cool and calm and humble—the kind of humility that comes from security. Even as a kid, every room he walked into, every situation he was in, people just knew that he was a powerful man. And they stepped back. Women could somehow sense his power and just wandered towards him. It was weird. He wasn't that big; he wasn't that tall. He wasn't good looking. But by doing absolutely nothing he commanded the attention of everyone in the room.

So what I saw was how this rich, powerful, successful father raised his son. I watched how he valued his son and how he invested his precious time in his son. This made his son precious, valuable. There seemed to be a direct correlation between the amount of time the father spent with his son and the amount of poise and confidence the son had.

And from that, I learned again that even to the very wealthy, the most important thing—and the thing that was more important than money or time—was the relationship the father made with his kids.

As one moves up Maslow's hierarchy of needs from physiological needs to safety needs, through love and belonging and esteem, to self-actualization and transcendence, one begins to understand that there are certain universal, objective values that are held in high esteem by successfully self-actualized families everywhere. These universal values are accepted across all cultures and throughout every society.

And the number one value, the object of the highest priority, the thing that's the most important, the thing that carries more value than land, diamonds or gold is family.

John

About 15 years ago, my wife and I were at a party. This party was thrown for some old friends of ours that were visiting from New Zealand. It was a pretty raucous party with a bunch of very wild 30-something hipsters. We were definitely the oldest couple there and we had two kids.

Our friend John and his wife had moved away to start a new life. He was a serious guy with an MBA from USC. When they got to New Zealand, he found a position with an international charity organization. John wanted to do something important. He wanted to make the world a better place. He quickly worked his way up the organization.

As I watched John move through the party, I could tell that something was wrong. He was smiling and talking, but I could tell that he was in the middle of some kind of existential crisis. I had been there before and I knew what that smelled like. I don't remember whether he came to me or I found him, but at one point we left the party and went for a walk.

John told me his troubles and I told him mine. He told me that he was really happy at work and that he felt he was making a real contribution. He was projecting his visions into the world and having a real impact. He told me that he was actually making the world a better place. I asked, "Then what's the problem? You don't look so good. Why are you so blue?"

He told me that his wife wanted to have children and that he was freaking out about it. He said that he was finally getting to the point in his career that he was having an impact. He was actually helping people, and he didn't want to put all that on hold to have kids.

I told him that I had experienced the same freak-out. I freaked out when my wife told me that she wanted to start trying to have a kid. I freaked out in a big way. I even left home for a while and went off for a long trek in the desert to think things through.

Now, I was about 15 years older than John and I had already been through what he was going through. I had two kids and I had been through a lot of the times and troubles that he was worried about. More importantly, I had been through the same existential crisis that he was going through at that very moment.

I realized that I knew what to do. I knew what to say. Here is what I told him.

The most important thing you can do to make the world a better place is to make better children.

Sure, you have an impact in your position at your job at Oxfam, but really you know that the true impact you have with the many people that you come in contact with is slight and fleeting. You might have a little impact in a short amount of time with a large number of people, but with a kid, with a daughter or son of your own, you can have a huge impact on one person.

If you want to make the world a better place, have kids.

If you want to make the world a better place, raise happy, healthy, smart kids that are able to question the standard view and see the world clearly.

If you want to make the world a better place, choose to have a purpose in your life. Raise your kids with purpose.

If you want to make the world a better place, teach your kids how to learn and raise your kids to be smarter than you. Build your kids into the kind of people that are able to create new ideas and invent new technologies. These technologies will save the world.

If you want to make the world a better place,

Make Better Children!

What is the best way to make a happy, healthy child?

What is the easiest thing you can do to raise a kid that is calm, secure, confident and empathetic?

Is there a simple way, an easy thing that you can do that will have a profound impact on your kid's demeanor and stance throughout the course of his life?

LESSON SEVEN

Sleep with your baby

This is another important thing that you can do for the long-term health, confidence, and happiness of your child.

Sleeping with your baby makes a huge difference in their long-term development.

If you look at all of the large mammal families on Planet Earth and you study how they sleep and how they put their babies to sleep, I think you will find that most of the time the babies fall asleep being cuddled by their mothers. From bears to baboons, from rhinos to orangutans, this is a very natural thing to do and a very homo sapiens thing to do. There are also some vital strategic reasons to do this. Sleeping with your baby keeps them calm and quiet. In the wild, this is important because it limits the exposure to nocturnal predators and other problems. For a human family, it is important because having a quiet, calm, sleeping baby gives the mother and the father more time to rest.

I understand that some people react to this idea intensely. Some people feel like the bed of the husband and wife is a sacred place. They feel that it is important to keep the bed private so that they can ensure the harmony of the marriage. They feel that the sanctity of the bed must be defended and protected. And they feel that bringing a baby into the couple's bed might destroy that sanctity. I understand this idea and I agree that it is important to maintain a close physical relationship with your spouse. But bringing the baby into your bed is so important that it is worth exploring a compromise.

Some people think that it is important to teach the child to be independent, self-calming and self-reliant. But I don't agree. An infant in the first year of life wants security more than anything else. It is important to set yourself in the mind of the child and try to view the world from the child's point of view. The child instinctively wants to know that it is safe and warm and fed and taken care of. Its senses are tuned to establish its physical wellbeing.

In the first days, weeks and months of life, the infant tests its environment and tunes its mind and strategy to fit its surroundings. The baby starts out cooing and smiling, hoping to establish the basic human contact with its mother and father. The baby's mind instinctively plays the tit-for-tat game presenting a happy, cute, loving display. If the baby receives loving, kind attention, in return it literally rewires its brain to be happy, calm and loving.

If, on the other hand, the baby feels cold, hungry, vulnerable or neglected, it will actually rewire its brain to take a more defensive posture. If the baby is laid down to sleep in a crib in a room alone and wakes up feeling vulnerable or neglected, it will feel scared and cry for its mother. Having this situation happen over and over again will literally change the way the baby's brain develops. The child will grow up to be more withdrawn, more defensive, less secure and less empathetic.

If, on the other hand, the baby stirs in the middle of the night and half-awake she blindly stretches to sense her space and senses that she is not alone and that she is protected by her big, strong, powerful mommy and daddy, she knows that she is safe. The baby will fall back asleep with the understanding that she is loved and cherished. The baby's brain will actually rewire itself. As the baby develops, it will be open and happy. The child will grow up to be more confident, more secure and more empathetic.

When you sleep with your baby, the baby sleeps better. Put the baby up next to you in bed, in between you and your wife, with your head, your baby's head and your wife's head at the same level. This way your baby can't roll out of bed or get tangled in the sheets. With your baby at the top of the bed, he or she will be safe and warm, and you will be able to keep a sense of your baby through the night.

Sometimes your baby will sleepily reach out and find your mouth with its hand. This is the sweetest thing. I wonder if babies do this just to make sure that you are there and you are still breathing. When you sleep with your baby, they sleep longer and deeper and you get more sleep as well.

When you sleep with your baby and your wife is nursing, feeding the baby is peaceful and easy. When your baby stirs at night, wakes up hungry and wants something to eat, instead of waking up, getting up and going into the next room, waking up your baby, taking them out of bed, holding your baby and nursing them, it is much easier for your wife to just roll over and give the baby a little snack. This way you don't have to wake up. Your wife doesn't have to stand up. And your baby doesn't have to fully wake to have a drink. It is another way for you, your wife and your baby to get a better, deeper sleep.

When you sleep with your baby in the same bed, the baby sleeps sounder, deeper and more peacefully. This brings the stress level of the whole family down and makes everybody's life a little easier.

And yes, there is more to it. When you sleep with your baby, their brain develops a different way. Sleeping all in the same bed is just a more secure way to be. It is just more mammalian. It gives your baby a kind of fundamental confidence that is hard to quantify. They grow up with a fundamental sense of security that permeates everything else they do. They stand up taller. They walk more confidently. They move into groups without hesitation. Giving your children this kind of tranquil, composed, unflappable foundation is extremely important and is without question one of the most important things you can do.

This gives your baby a deeply secure sense of confidence. Everything you can do to give your child that kind of security is very important. I know it sounds almost too simple, but sleeping with your baby, from day one, is an important way to give your children a foundation derived from a secure connection to their mother, their father, and their family.

There is a way to make a happy, healthy child.

There is a way to raise a kid that is calm, secure, confident and empathetic.

Bring your baby into your bed and sleep with your baby resting in between you and your wife.

This is the simplest and easiest thing you can do to radically change the rest of your children's lives.

Sleeping with your baby will have a profound impact on your child's demeanor and stance throughout the course of his life.

Superpower #7

Physical Security

How many times during your daily life do you walk into a situation with complete composure? How many times do you, during your day, face a new or uncertain situation? Of those times, how many times are you cool, calm, tranquil and composed?

Let's say this morning you get a call from your biggest client and they are not happy. Let's say that they are screaming at you about this or that and they want to see you in their office in two hours to present an update of your current project in front of the board of directors.

Is this a problem? Does your heart rate go up? Do you get nervous? Or are you cool? This might be an opportunity for you to shine in front of the Board or make a fool of yourself and be booted down. What do you do?

You might be on top of the project. You might be ahead of schedule and under budget, but you still get spooked. You start to sweat and you start to tremble. You understand that even the appearance of nervousness will signal weakness. And that understanding makes you even more nervous. A stutter or fumble here might cost you the position or the job. You can't be nervous.

You've seen people that can do this. You've heard about people that are always cool under pressure. You've seen them in movies. You might even know a guy that seems to be able to keep his head while everyone around him is losing theirs— the NFL quarterback, the Navy fighter pilot, the ER trauma surgeon.

You know that the guys that are cool under pressure are perceived as more competent and proficient.

That's what you need to be. That's what you want your kids to be. How does this happen? How do these guys learn how to thrive in high-stress environments?

This is what this Superpower gives your kids—an inner sense of cool, a deep foundational sense of composure, not the appearance of tranquility but the base state of tranquility.

How do you give your kids an underlying sense of calm?

How do you grow children that are composed and cool in every situation?

How do you give your kids a sense of security that is so deep and foundational that their base state is one of tranquility?

Sleeping with your baby is that best way to do that.

It is simple. It is almost too easy. And it makes everyone's life a little easier.

Sleep with your babies and raise happy, healthy, cool children.

Uncle Ben Parker, in a Spiderman comic said,

"With great power comes great responsibility."

I would like to turn that upside down and say,

"With great responsibility comes great power."

Would you like to feel that power?

Would you like to know what it feels like to hold great responsibility?

Until you have a kid, you have no idea what that means.

LESSON EIGHT

How to feed a baby

I think big, fat babies are the best. If you try to think about all of the changes a little baby has to go through in the first six months of life, it is amazing. The baby has to double its weight and double its size. At the same time, the baby's brain is exploding. The baby has to finish wiring up all the connections between all of the different systems in its body. When the baby is first born, it doesn't really have control of any of its systems. Its eyes can't focus, its arms fly around, its legs kick and its tongue seems to be some kind of alien creature living inside your kid's mouth. All of these subsystems have to be connected and coordinated.

To do this the baby needs a lot of energy. It needs to eat all the time. And just like any other baby—a baby bird, a little puppy or a baby dolphin, for example—they need to eat something at least every two hours. Your baby is going to need a lot to eat. Make sure you can make that happen.

The more you can get your baby to eat in the first year of life, the bigger brain your kid will have its whole life long. It is important to understand that brain cells are basically modified fat cells. So big, fat babies are the best. A big, chubby baby with "Michelin Man" arms and legs is the ideal.

I would try to feed our babies all the time. That is not always easy, and sometimes it's just not possible. Here are a few things you can do to help.

First things first—when the baby is born, within a minute or two, give the baby to the mommy so it can have something to drink. Sometimes the mommy's milk hasn't come in yet, but it helps to make that connection.

If the mommy's milk hasn't come in yet, give the baby formula. A lot of people don't like this idea. People like to strive for an all-natural child, but, hey, it is important to make sure the priorities are set straight. The very top priority is the health and well-being of the baby. Sometimes it is easy to get caught up in the process and miss out on the goal. And the goal here is to have a big, strong, smart, healthy, happy baby.

If the baby is hungry and the mommy doesn't have any milk, don't wait a day to see what happens. Get the baby something to eat now. The first day, the first hours are very important. Take care of the baby first. If the mommy doesn't have any milk, make sure you have a bottle with some warm formula as a backup.

Continually feed your baby all through the first two years. Yes, we breastfed our babies, but I never felt shy about supplementing mommy's milk. Give the baby what it needs all the time. If it wants mommy and she's around, great. If you're out of mommy's milk, get some formula.

One of the things that we did to cope with mommy being away all day was to build up a large selection of mommy's milk in the freezer.

I was working at home all day, and my wife had to be up at UCLA working at school. I was trying to start a new business, and my wife was pursuing her Ph.D. I had invented a new kind of bicycle, and she was doing a large research study on elementary schools.

Anyway, I was at home all day and my wife was away. We wanted to feed our baby mommy's milk. We just wanted to. We knew that there are all kinds of reasons to raise your kid on breast milk—better weight gain, higher immune function, greater connection between mommy and baby, higher IQ. But in the end, we just wanted to feed baby mommy's milk.

To make that work, while Mommy was away she would collect her breast milk and save it for the next day. My wife would go to school every day with an elaborate system of a pump, a cooler and a bunch of ice. She would sneak away and hide in a closet somewhere near her office and pump her milk and save it in an assortment of small baby bottles. She would adorn each bottle with a piece of tape with the date so we could keep everything straight. Then she would store the bottles in a small cooler packed full of ice. When she got home every day, I would add these bottles to our growing inventory of mommy's milk stacked up in the freezer.

Each time my daughter got hungry, I would pick a bottle out of the freezer, thaw it out, warm it up and feed it to her. It was wild seeing all these different bottles in the fridge. The milk in each bottle was different. The color was different. The volume was different. The translucency was different. We figured that difference mostly depended on what I had made for dinner the night before. Whatever Mommy had eaten the previous day changed the way the milk was made the next day. You could clearly see the difference in each bottle of milk.

Well, that day that my daughter was crying, I had selected a bottle of milk that was a little rosy in color. It was dark and kind of pinkish brown. My daughter drank it but didn't like it. She tried it, but after a while, she spit it out. She was hungry, so she tried it again, but after she tasted it she started to cry. She cried and cried and cried. I didn't know what to do.

As it turned out, two nights before we had gone out to dinner. My wife had ordered some spicy Mexican dish. I think it was mole. Yes, I'm sure it was the mole. I never liked chocolate on my burritos, but my wife loves it. Anyway, the next day my wife pumped out her milk at school, and the following day I tried to feed that milk to my daughter. And, wouldn't you know it, as it turns out my daughter didn't like the mole either. My daughter didn't like spicy Mexican food. It upset her stomach and gave her fast poop. It took me a while to put two and two together, but after we figured that out, we learned to either stop eating Mexican food or just throw the brown milk away the next day.

Here's the thing. That day while I was desperately trying to figure out how to calm my daughter down, I did everything

I thought I knew how to do. I fed her and burped her. I changed her and changed her clothes. I changed the oil and rotated the tires. But nothing helped. She just kept crying. She probably cried for four hours. I held her and swayed her. I carried her and bounced her. I sang to her and coddled her. But nothing helped. She just cried and cried. The bad mole milk just had to make its way through her system. Then, after a while, it did. My daughter had a huge poop and she felt better. Well, she was relieved and I felt a lot better.

While I was holding her and cooing to her after she had stopped crying, I noticed something strange. I looked at her and she looked at me. She knew that I had been trying to help and I think she was grateful. She looked deep into my eyes. And I looked back. It was wild. We just gazed at each other. It really began to freak me out. It was frightening.

Having a child is like nothing you've ever felt.

I know people say this all the time.

I know dads say this all the time.

But until you've done it, until you've had a child, you can't possibly feel what I'm talking about.

Holding your child triggers deep primordial feelings and emotions that are unavailable to you until you hold your child. These are emotions that have been buried in your source code for literally millions of years. We may not have been humans back then, but the design code was being written into our wetware through a massively costly and expensive process of trial and error where the cost was blood and the expense was time. Where the trial was how to love your baby and an error led to death.

Billions and billions and billions of simple creatures died before that had a chance to breed. And each one of these deaths had an impact on who you are, how you think, how your brain is built and how your mind works.

Still with all of the science available to us now, we have absolutely no idea how this works. Oh yeah, the scientists say they are getting close to figuring the human mind out, but they have been saying that for decades. They have no idea. These instructions are hard-wired deep, deep, deep into the architectures of our brain, and they are triggered only when specific actions occur.

These actions light up some of the oldest, deepest subroutines in our mind, and these processes manifest themselves in the feelings and emotions that you feel when you hold, not just any baby, but your baby, your child, your offspring.

And get ready. When it happens to you, it will freak you out. You won't know where the feelings come from. You won't understand the depth of the emotion. The feeling is kind of dark and foreboding. It triggers a kind of papa bear, guttural grunt.

And when you make that grunt, you'll know that you are a father.

This is really the first time this happened to me. I was holding my infant daughter and she was looking at me, not through me, but into me. And I felt it. And I made that papa bear grunt.

A sound came out of me and it scared me.

I was like, "What the—? What was that?"

And I knew right then. I just knew.

It scared me. It scared me because I didn't understand where these feelings were coming from. It scared me because I didn't expect it or didn't see it coming. I thought at the moment that it was something else.

Every person has an inner person that is completely themselves. Every person has a private part of themselves that they keep completely separate and private to themselves. There is a part of you that is totally you that you keep for yourself. It is the part of you that you talk to when you're talking to yourself. That part you keep guarded. You keep that part separate. You don't share that part with anybody.

To be precise, most people have a wall that separates their true self from their innermost self, and they don't even realize that this wall is there. You keep this wall there as a defense, as protection, survival, self-preservation—it's a subconscious thing. And it's partly a bandwidth thing. Most of your innermost thoughts are pre-linguistic. They are feelings without words. They are thoughts and emotions that form who you are, and there's really no way to communicate these ideas to anyone else outside your head. So you keep this part separate and private.

This is a natural thing and everybody does it. Everybody keeps a wall around their innermost self.

And here I was, holding my child, and she was looking right into me, right through the wall, right at my innermost self.

And it was scary.

I think most guys I know, most dads I know get to this point and stop. They get to this point and it freaks them out. They feel vulnerable, defenseless and weak. They feel shy. They feel scared. And they don't know why. They are not accustomed to having someone, anyone, look past their defenses, past their inner wall. It shakes them up.

So they stop and reinforce the wall. They build a wall between themselves and their kids. I see that as an act of cowardice. I see dads do this because they are selfish and scared. I see dads do this because they haven't taken the time to define their own personal values. They don't know or understand what is truly important in life, so they retreat back into themselves and hunker down into their bunker.

I didn't do that. For me, it was the other way around. For me, the papa bear took over. My papa bear instinct kicked in and I knew what to do.

I knew right then that I was a father. I knew that I was a daddy. And I knew that it was time to step up and go –

All in.

I decided there and then to go all in, to be committed, to commit myself to being a dad.

To love my kids and be there for them –

No matter what.

And this is what you should do too.

With great responsibility comes great power.

It is time to step up.

It is time to take the responsibility.

It is time to commit yourself to being the best father you can be.

It is time to become a Superdaddy.

Superpower #8

Power

At the risk of sounding periphrastic, Power is the real Superpower.

You never really love someone until you have a child.

You love your family and you love your woman, but it's different when you have a child. Something changes. It's just more. It's more intense. It is more profound. It is a different, deeper kind of love. It is a kind of love that you have never felt before. And until you have a child, you have not had that feeling. Your life becomes bigger, more intense, more serious, and more substantial. You now have skin in the game. You now have a tie to the future. You now have an obligation to the planet and the destiny of mankind. You feel this when you have a child.

It takes courage to accept this obligation.

It takes courage to love someone that deeply.

It takes a lot of courage to show someone who you really are.

It takes courage to allow someone else to see your insecurities and weaknesses.

It takes courage to sense your humanity.

It takes the greatest amount of courage to accept this amount of responsibility.

But then, "With great responsibility comes great power."

It is time for you to step up and accept this responsibility.

Love your baby.

Do you want to have influence?

Do you want to project your legacy into the future?

Do you want to design a system of empowerment

that builds generational wisdom?

Do you want your life to have meaning?

LESSON NINE

Never punk your kid

Everybody loves to play with their babies. I love to play with my babies.

Playing with your children is one of the funniest (yes, that's a word), most satisfying, most gratifying things a daddy can ever do. Whether it is chasing your toddler around the yard, trying to hit your son's fastball, following your kid down a ski slope in the powder through the trees, or mountain biking off the back of some mountain, there is just something about it that cannot be put to words.

Especially when they kick your ass. One of the greatest days in a daddy's life is the day when your son or daughter beats you at your sport. Be it in a race like running or swimming, in a game like poker or chess, or when they discover the literary significance of a visual element in a movie that you hadn't caught. It is a moment that stands in your life like nothing else. Although the first time my daughter beat me at chess (I think she was only six), it was just humiliating.

If you are a purposeful parent, if your goal is to make better children, if you want to give your kids a better life than you have had, then to watch them best you at anything is a cherished moment. It is a moment of glory. It is a rung on the ladder of success. It is a small, incremental validation of your progress. And it should be celebrated.

It is a succession of small wins, of incremental successes that build confidence. And it is confidence that allows your children to reach even higher toward greater goals. And if your goal is to have your children achieve bigger things than you have achieved, then to watch them beat you is the best feeling ever.

So—here's the deal. Don't trick them.

One day I was playing with my daughter. We were living in an 80-year-old barn in Eagle Rock, California. After being evicted from our UCLA apartment, my wife found an incredible place up near Pasadena. It was an old barn built out of river rock and telephone poles on a quarter acre lot on the side of a hill. It had a 30 foot, open beam ceiling painted with German stencils. It was like living in Hansel and Gretel's castle.

It was magical. My wife would get up and go to work each day, and I had a work-from-home job where I spent most of my time on the phone or on the internet. I also got to stay home and take care of my kids.

We woke up every morning and got out of the same big bed. I would get up and make my wife coffee and my daughter breakfast. My wife would get ready for work, and I would change the diapers. It was a magical time.

One day, after my wife had gone to work, I was playing with my daughter on the bed when I did a stupid thing. She was probably two or thereabouts. It's funny. When I was doing it, I didn't think it was a stupid thing. I thought that this was just the way that daddies play with their daughters. We were playing a game where she would stand up on the bed and pretend to fall. She would stand up. Then she would look at me. Then she would fall face-first, towards me, and I would catch her. Then she would laugh and I would laugh and we would do it over again. She would fall and I would catch her; then she would fall and I would catch her.

This is before she had any words. Most of our communication was nonverbal. So she didn't have any way verbally to tell me what she was thinking, but at this level, we didn't need any words. We both knew what each other was thinking.

So, we would play this game. She would fall and I would catch her; then she would fall and I would catch her. Except, this one time I thought it would be funny if I didn't catch her. She fell and I didn't catch her. I don't know why I thought that would be funny. Maybe it was some kind of cultural normality of what a "joke" is—a prank—to punk someone. People think it's funny. Well, it's not funny. This one time, when I didn't catch my baby, she fell and started to cry. She fell on the bed, so she didn't get hurt physically, but the damage was done. I had broken our trust.

She looked up at me with tears in her eyes, and she said to me (without words), "What was that? Why did you do that?" She cried and cried. I tried to get an instant do-over to show her that everything was ok, but she wasn't having it. The trust had been broken and she didn't want to play anymore.

I felt horrible.

So—here's the deal. Don't betray the trust that you have with your kids. Don't trick them into thinking that you are there to protect them and then not protect them. When children are very young, they need to stand on a secure foundation of trust. They need to have faith that you are there to keep them safe and protect them. It is from this secure foundation that their minds are safe to develop and blossom to their highest potential.

You want to play with your kids. You want to compete with your kids. You want to race against your children. This is done to make them better. Don't cheat them. Work toward providing a secure environment for them to develop in. Let them know that they can trust you with everything in every situation. Make sure that you let them know through your actions that you are on the same team, moving in the same direction, towards the same goals.

This is the best way to build a strong foundation for your children.

Now let's talk about the opposite of that.

What happens when you do punk your kids? What happens when you purposely remove trust from your relationship with your baby?

111

When you build trust with your baby, they grow, and their mind grows, in an environment of safety and security. They grow up subconsciously knowing that they are safe, that you hold their best interest paramount and that they can count on you to protect them. This deeply-held knowing of security enables them to grow in a different way. It is like growing a plant in a bed of horse poo in a temperate hothouse vs. growing the plant in sandy soil in the frozen desert. The hothouse plant is going to grow up bigger, stronger, faster. The frozen desert plant is going to grow slower and smaller.

There is a tradeoff. The smaller desert plant is going to grow up tougher.

Let's say that you want tougher, meaner kids. Let's say that you think that tougher, meaner people are more successful, so you choose to raise your kids within a hostile environment. If you build an atmosphere in your household that is, like a frozen desert, brutal and caustic, you will probably end up with tougher, meaner kids. These kids might be able to survive in more brutal and caustic environments, but you will have to pay a price. The price, in this case, will be your kids will waste most of their lives making the same mistakes that you have made.

Once you betray their trust in you, they will no longer trust you. This one little thing will have small consequences in the beginning. They won't listen to you. They won't take directions from you. They will not be able to accept your coaching or advice. This is kind of cute when they are two, but when they get to be 13, it is a brutal, heart-crushing reality. Sure, they will be more independent and more set and resolute, but you won't be able to help them.

One of the five greatest inventions of humankind is abstract learning, the transfer of knowledge from person to person. The reason humankind has advanced so far and so fast is that an old man can share his wisdom with a younger man. This one tool has made it possible for the younger man to not have to waste his time making the same mistakes that the older man has made. Because of this one thing, the younger man can use the lessons of the older man to use his time to gain even greater wisdom.

This is the thing you give away when you punk your baby. If you punk your baby, they will shut you down. They will stop listening to you. And they will stop trusting you. By the time they get to be 13, they will be lost to you. You will no longer be able to have any input or leverage, and they will end up living the same dumbass, boring life that you have led. They won't be able to learn from your mistakes because they can't hear you. They can't hear you because they don't trust you. And they don't trust you because you punked them when they were babies.

Never punk your kids—never make them the butt of your joke. Never make fun of them or belittle them. Belittlement and humiliation is a pain that won't go away. If you do this when they're young, they will not trust you or listen to you when they get older.

If you punk your kids, your family will not progress. Your kids and their kids and their kids will be stuck living the same mistakes over and over and over again.

So if you want to be a Superdaddy and raise Superchildren, if you want to set your family on a path to become a Superfamily, a family that can share generational wisdom and become bigger and better and stronger and more powerful, then raise your children in a safe, secure, loving environment. Construct an environment in which they know that they can trust you and they know that you are holding their best interest at the top of your value pyramid. Raise your children in this loving environment, and they will listen to you and take direction from you and learn from your wisdom while they are teenagers, the most crucial times of their lives.

You can have influence.

You can project your legacy into the future.

Begin now designing a system of empowerment that builds generational wisdom.

Design meaning into your life to be passed forward to your great-grandchildren's future.

Start now by building a loving, secure environment in which you raise your children.

Never punk your kids.

Become a Superdaddy.

And help save the world.

Superpower #9

Generational Wisdom

Great families are made by passing along generational wisdom.

If you have a kid that's a junior in high school, you are probably helping your child fill out college applications this year. As you run through the extensive questionnaire, you will come upon one interesting question. "Did your mother or father, grandmother or grandfather attend this university?"

They call this "legacy." All of the Ivy League schools and all of the top universities in the country ask this question. The universities ask this question because they are trying to assess the viability of the candidate. They want to know what chance your potential student will have in completing his degree. They want to try to guess in advance what percentage chance your kid will have in finishing school in four years.

Each of the big schools has been keeping track, keeping score and compiling the records of tens of thousands or hundreds of thousands of students for tens or even hundreds of years. To keep their dropout rate low and their completion rate high, they want to accept only the kids that have the best chances of finishing their degree on time. By analyzing the data, the universities know that one of the best predictors of future success is the family structure of the applicant. i.e., if the dad or the grandpa, mom or grandma of the applicant was a successful student, chances are that the applicant will also be a successful student.

The universities know from decades of research that successful families teach their children how to be successful. If the mom or dad of the applicant is a success, then there is a really good chance that the kid will be successful too.

This is called generational wisdom. This is where the elders of the family are able to pass along critical information to the younglings. This is where successful grandparents teach their kids how to be successful and successful parents teach their kids the secrets of their grandparents.

But this can only happen if you as a parent have created a family environment of security and trust.

And this can only happen if your kids will listen to you.

And your kids will not listen to you if you have punked them when they were young.

Become a Superdaddy.

Build a family environment of security and trust.

Pass along generational wisdom to your kids and

Raise Super heroes.

Would you like to grant your children the power of deep mammalian empathy?

Would you like to be able to give your children the ability to have an intuitive sense of the positive or negative intentions of the people they come in contact with?

Would you like to build in them the ability to instantly read the emotional state of anyone?

If you could, would you like to give them a kind of empathetic telepathy?

LESSON TEN

Get a dog

There are a lot of good reasons to have a dog.

Having a pet in the house changes your child's fundamental understanding of nature. When you have a pet, your baby learns from experience about life, nature, compassion, and death.

All that stuff that they say about dogs is true. Having a dog makes life more fun. Dogs are always happy to see you. They don't care if you've had a bad day or a bad year. They don't care if you're hurt or broken. They don't care if someone breaks your heart or you've been stuck in traffic. They just want to be with you and be happy.

This kind of cheeriness rubs off on your kids. Having a dog in the house makes things better.

Raising Superheroes is hard work. There is a lot of stress. There might be stress at work or stress at home, but your dog doesn't care. It just wants to play. And playing with your dog can help redistribute the stress within your family structure and take some of the pressure off.

And there's more. Studies show that kids raised in households with dogs have a stronger immune system and get sick less often. This turns out to be a big deal when your kids start going to school. My kids didn't get sick much (knock on wood). When your kids start going to daycare or pre-K or however you start, it is really crazy. It is like a giant germ-fest in there where all of the kids bring everybody's germs to school all the time. All of the kids are coming down with all kinds of croup and crud, sneezes, and sniffles. This is messy and inconvenient, but it is not necessarily a bad thing. This kind of exposure to these kinds of petty sicknesses builds the kids' immune systems and makes them stronger in the long run.

And we were lucky. Our kids were pretty strong. We didn't have to keep them home from school very often. When the other kids were out sick, our kids just kept on plugging away. If your kid is out of school, you have to be out of work. This is a negative amplifying feedback loop that just gets worse and worse and bigger and bigger. The more they're out, the more you miss, the more stress gets added to the system. The more stress in the system, the lower your immune response. The lower the immune response, the more you get sick. The more you get sick, the more work and school you miss. The more school you miss, the more stress gets added to the system.

Having dogs in the house—with all of their dirty, messy crud and crap—helped my kids build a strong immune system and keep healthier over a longer time.

Next, kids get to see first-hand what it takes to take care of something. You have to feed your dog and clean up after your dog. You have to walk your dog and play with your dog. You have to give your dog a bath and take it to the vet. The process of taking care of a dog teaches your kids, on an intuitive level, about the process of life. In fact, having a dog teaches your kids about all kinds of cycles. And learning about all of these cycles are healthy lessons to learn about their own natural health and their own life.

Start with a puppy. Get a dog when your kids are babies. Bring the dog into your home and make it part of the family. As early as you can, give your children the responsibility of taking care of the dog. It is their dog. Let them name the dog and take ownership of it. Let them know that it is their dog and they are responsible for another living being. Teach them how to feed their dog, and make sure that they understand that if they don't feed their dog and give water to their dog, their dog will go hungry.

These are chores, like on a farm. Farmers deeply and intuitively understand their responsibilities and obligations. They have a deep connection to the natural world. They know that their animals depend on them. They know that if they don't feed their animals, their animals will starve.

I've spent many summers on our farm in Iowa, and I've learned how to do chores. I remember specifically as a nine-year-old kid playing all day with my cousins thinking, I'm hungry and tired and hot and sticky. I don't want to go down to the barn and feed the pigs. I want to eat dinner and hang out in the house. My Uncle Everett screamed at me, "Who do you think you are? Those poor animals are hot and tired and hungry. If you don't feed them, they won't get fed. Get your lazy ass down there and do your chores." This is one of the ways I learned compassion. This is the way to learn responsibility and obligation.

When your kids get to be toddlers and they're big enough to hold the dog and pet the dog, they will learn about compassion and tenderness. They will make a connection between the way they are touched and treated and the way they touch and treat their dog. This is an important physical, kinetic lesson to learn. It brings them closer to the natural world. It builds compassion, empathy and a deeper sense of what it is to be human.

When you sit with a dog on the couch, it's a big deal. The dog will run in and jump on you and want to be with you. This forces your kids out of their internal space. This forces them out of their own head. Sure, you could give your kid an iPad or some other device to occupy their time and use up their attention, but that isn't going to help them be better or get better in any way. Giving your kids some kind of electrical device to play with isn't going to help them become human.

But if you sit with a dog on the couch, you start to understand what it is like to be with another creature, how to touch something and how to be tender. You learn through intimate feedback what is too hard or too rough. You sense what other creatures feel. Your kids will learn empathy and compassion. They will feel compassion for the other creatures of the world, and this will help them learn how to be more human.

And when your kids grow up, when they learn to be with someone else, when they need to bond with another human in a close, physical way, they will have a huge head start if they have lived with a dog. They will have learned how to be tender from their time spent on the couch with their pet.

Another thing that your kids learn from a dog is the interplay between loneliness and happiness. Everyone has to spend time alone. Everyone has to learn how to be alone and what it's like to be alone. Your time on earth isn't full of experience and fun. Your time isn't always completely used up with excitement and challenge. Many, many hours of life are spent in lonely boredom—where you don't really have anyone to talk to or anyone to be with. Being in this position is a painful but necessary part of life. It is important to learn about loneliness and teach your child that sometimes it is okay to be alone. It is also important to teach your child that they can find ways to fight loneliness. It is kind of a Yin-Yang thing—without loneliness, there is no happiness. And sometimes the Yang to this Yin is to commune with another creature, to have a dog.

Another thing, a dog's life is lived in fast forward. They grow up fast, they mature quickly, they get old and they die. This may be sad, but it is important for everyone to see this process unfold. Having a dog brings your kids closer to nature and closer to a natural way of living. It gives your kids a firsthand, fundamental view of the cycle of life.

It's time to level up -

Most of the brain activity that goes on in a person's head happens on a subconscious level. All of the feelings, emotions, and intuitions that you feel are formed within wetware that isn't directly connected to your conscious. Maybe up to eighty percent of your brain's activity is algorithms and subroutines that are running in a part of your brain that you have absolutely no awareness of. These are the thoughts that present themselves as feelings, emotions, and intuitions.

These feelings, emotions, and intuitions develop in lower levels of your brain, your animal brain, your lizard brain. I feel that it is important to be aware of these mental animal traits. You need to learn to be the best animal you can be before you can be fully human.

And the best time to do this is when you are a small child.

Living with a dog, communing with animals helps develop these lower animal mental processes early in life. Living with a dog enables your children to develop a deep animalistic empathy that is very hard to quantify but becomes obvious and powerful as they grow older. This empathy is the ability to commune with other creatures. It is the ability to emotionally put yourself in the other creature's position. It is the ability to imagine what it is like to be that other creature and feel the emotions that other creatures might be feeling.

This empathy becomes a powerful tool as your children grow older. With this empathy, they will be able to sense when a person is being honest with them or when a person is trying to deceive them. They will be able to sense instantly and intuitively, on a gut level, if the person they are talking to is a real person or is some kind of narcissistic psychopath.

This powerful tool can be developed very early in life and is best developed by living and playing with animals. And this intuition will become a tool that your children will use the rest of their lives.

Get a dog when your kids are young and raise the dog as part of your family.

You can give your children deep mammalian empathy.

You can grant your children the ability to have an intuitive sense of other people's intentions.

Your children will be able to instantly read the emotional state of anyone they meet.

Give your children the Superpower of empathetic telepathy.

Get a dog.

Superpower #10

Empathetic Telepathy

With this power, your children will be able to quickly assess the mental and emotional states of the people they come close enough to touch. They will be able to intuitively sense the positive and negative emotions that run underneath every interaction and every conversation. They will be able to sense if they are dealing with an honest person or if they are being deceived. They will be able to feel if the person that they are talking to has positive or negative intentions. They will be able to guide their lives away from negative people and situations. And they will be able to guide their lives toward positive people and many more positive, optimistic and constructive situations.

Empathetic telepathy — the ability to read the inner feelings of, or to project your inner feelings on to others.

Here I present a way to learn empathetic telepathy and to teach empathetic telepathy to your children.

You start by thinking about it. You start by making a space for these ideas in your mind. Begin by concentrating on this communication and recognizing how you are thinking and feeling.

Keep this idea present in your thoughts every time you touch another creature. Create a vision in your mind of the ideas that you are trying to communicate. Do this every time with every animal. You look into their eyes and take a moment to imagine how that animal might be feeling, and you create a space in your mind where you can communicate with that being.

Every time you touch another creature, create a string of thoughts in this space, a visual representation of what you are trying to say.

With a little practice with a dog, you will notice an amazing effect. Try this for a while and see if it works.

Whenever you touch your puppy, think in your head what you want your puppy to feel. For instance, if you want your puppy to calm down, you first imagine why the puppy is excited. It might be because the puppy is feeling nervous and insecure. In that case, you pet them and silently project to your pet, "Calm down puppy. Everything is okay. Everyone loves you and everything will be okay."

This will have an amazing, calming effect.

If you want to play and go for a run, you might just need to look at your puppy and think, Let's go for a walk. Your dog will sense this instantly and run and get his leash.

Or maybe you go for a walk and you absentmindedly walk into a sketchy place. You look at your dog and think, We are in danger; you need to protect me. Your dog will feel your anxiety and they will become attentive and aggressive.

Now, this doesn't happen every time and it doesn't happen with every animal. You have to practice these techniques for many years to get proficient. Some people are really good at this. Some people are called horse whisperers because they can communicate with their horses without words. Some hunters have dogs that they guide with just a wink, a nod, and a whistle. And some people use these techniques to control everyone they work with. If you practice, you can learn to do this and can get really good at it.

This connection, the psychic connection, between babies and puppies usually happens automatically. Here is a way you can talk about it, initiate it and enhance it.

When you first introduce your baby to your puppy, tell both your baby and your puppy to be gentle and kind.

When they get old enough to understand, maybe one or two years old, you will want to teach them a new game. I call this the "Feelings Game."

The Feelings Game is kind of like the old game of telephone, where you sit in a circle with your friends and whisper stories to each other in a loop. The first person whispers a short sentence in the ear of the person next to them. This short story is passed from person to person around the circle.

With the Feelings Game, you do the same thing, but you do it with just you, your child and their puppy, and you do it with feelings. You stroke your child's hair and you pass your feelings from you to your child. Then you tell your child to do the same to their puppy. Tell them to pet their puppy and try to pass the same feelings that they feel for them to their puppy.

Wait for a time when your puppy is calm. Then you get your child to sit with their puppy on their lap.

You hold your child on your lap while your child is holding their puppy on their lap.

You tell your child to close their eyes. Then tell them to concentrate on how they feel.

You close your eyes and imagine this space. You hold your child on your lap and you imagine the feelings of love and attentiveness. You connect these feelings with unspoken words that you say to yourself in your head. You tell your child how you feel, but you don't say it. You visualize it and you feel it. You connect these feelings to colors and emotions, but you don't talk about it; you just visualize it in your mind as you hold your child on your lap.

At first, you want to do this without spoken words. There is a reason for this. The part of your brain that controls language is a major control center for your mind. Once you speak the words, your brain and your child's brain automatically access the language center in your brain. Once you engage this mechanism, the language control center automatically overrides and disengages other parts of your mind.

I encourage you to try and step through this process several times with feelings first before you engage language. It is difficult to do, so it will take some practice.

After you have sat quietly for a while with your child, the next step is to bring words into the communication.

Tell your child how you feel as you hold them.

Then ask your child to describe to you how they feel.

Then tell your child to pet their puppy, and tell them to try to give the puppy the same feelings that they have as you hold them.

Then ask them to describe how they think the puppy is feeling.

Like in the Telephone Game, where you communicate an idea from one person to the next, in the Feelings Game you pass your feelings from you to your child and from your child to their pet. First, you communicate your feelings without words, just by holding them. Then you ask your child to pass their feelings from you to them to their puppy. Then you tell your child to try to imagine what the puppy is feeling.

As you hold your child, you ask them to concentrate on how it feels. Then tell them to pet their puppy's hair and try to get them to give the same feelings to their puppy as they feel themselves.

The Feelings Game is an exercise that you can use to strengthen the bond between you and your children and the bond between your children and their pets. It is also a way that you can teach and strengthen your child's emotional telepathy, a Superpower that they will use for the rest of their lives.

Can you build success into your kids?

Can you install systems of logic and reason into your children at an early age?

Can you teach your kids about self-reliance and personal responsibility?

Can you ignite their creative, inventive spark?

Can you teach your kids to play offense and attack?

Can you teach your kids to assert their freewill?

LESSON ELEVEN

*Never talk to your kid, especially your daughter,
like a baby*

Your kids develop and grow using you as their model.

They look to you as their perfect form.

They will mimic everything you do.

They will copy the way you walk, your posture and the
way you hold yourself, and the way you gesture and move
your hands. They will notice and copy everything, down to
and including your emotions, intentions and subtle intuitions,
even if they don't know what you're doing, what it means or
how to put your actions into context.

It is important to recognize this fact and act accordingly.

This is the time to instill in your children the
fundamentals of freewill.

We live in a loud world. I come from a loud family. My
kids are loud.

One time years ago when my daughter was maybe three,
some old friends stopped by for dinner. As usual for an
impromptu dinner party at our house, friends would come

over mid-afternoon; our kids would play and we would think about what we wanted to eat. Then we would jump in the car, drive down to the local market and buy whatever we thought looked good. My friend and I hadn't seen each other in a while and we were catching up. We wanted to continue our conversation, so we decided that we should all go down to the store, but the dads should take one car and the mommies and babies should take another car.

My friend and I took off. Engaged in conversation, we got to the store, parked our car and went inside. We moved through the store talking about some deep, important something and looking for what we wanted to eat. It was a busy Saturday evening and the store was crowded. Maybe twenty minutes into our shopping spree, we were in the very back of a large grocery store looking for sour cream or something and my friend asks, "Hey, where are the girls?" I said, "Oh, they're not here yet."

My friend laughed and said, "How do you know? They must be here by now."

"Oh, they're not here. We are the loud family. If my kid was in this store, we would hear her."

Right then my daughter comes crashing in the front door of the store screaming at the top of her lungs, "Hey everybody. We're here!" as if to tell everybody else in the store that it's okay to start the party now.

We were in the opposite corner of the store, mind you. My daughter was here and we knew it. My friend just busted up. We both laughed our brains out. We both thought it was funny that our kids were so unencumbered that they could just scream out in a crowded grocery store. And that's the way I liked it.

What happens in your local grocery store is a telling micro-culture of what's happening in the family structures around the country. You can watch what goes on within an inter-family unit sort of like a hidden urban sociologist. The family is there getting their business done. They have a chore to do. They need to buy some food. It is usually later in the day, after work, when the parents are tired and the kids are hungry. This is a great time to watch people interact and study how they manage their families.

I call these places semi-public. Oh sure, you're out in public, but in a way, you're kind of in a private little family cocoon. You're there getting personal business done—you're working on your own agenda. You know that there are other people there, but you're kind of oblivious to them. They've got things to do, you've got things to do and everybody's doing their own thing. Once in a while, you run into someone you know, but even then it's kind of awkward. "Hi, Betty. How's it going? Broke his leg again? That sucks. Ya, give me a call. Let's get together soon." And then you move on, working your way down the aisles and checking the things off of your scavenger list. You're in public, but you're in your own world.

From the outside, our family must have looked like a hot mess. My kids were usually screaming and running all over the place. And I was usually going about my business of running around and screaming.

I would always let my kids down out of the kid seat in the grocery cart. Sometimes they would be tired and they would want to ride along, and sometimes they would want to sit in the seat because—hey, it's called a kid's seat. Maybe it's for kids? Or maybe they see other kids in it and think that this is how it's supposed to be, but that usually only lasts about three minutes. Then they want to get down and run around. I would let them. I would lift them out of the seat, set them on their feet and let them go.

There are a few things going on here. The first is—"Hey, I trust you." You are telling your kid, even your two-year-old, that you trust them and that you think that they are good enough, smart enough and big enough to have this freedom. Second, you have got to let them go so that they can learn their own personal safety bubble. A grocery store is a great place to do this, by the way. They are out in public, but they are still inside the relatively safe space of the store.

My kids would usually stay close to me, shy and quiet to start, hugging my leg or riding on the cart, but after a while, they would see something they like and venture out on their own. They would eventually find the toy section, the candy section or the cold cereal section, and they would find something that they really, really, really wanted to have. They would pick it up and show it to me and baby mime (baby mime, i.e., at this point your kid is too young to have words or complete sentences so she acts out what she wants) "Please, please, I have to have this." I would tell them that they can't have that. To put it back and we have to move on. They would put up a fuss and the battle would begin.

And this is really my point here. Don't talk to your kid like a baby. Don't start the negotiation with baby talk. Don't say booboo, baby, gootchy goo, blah, blah, blah. Don't talk down to them. Don't talk in a high, squeaky, child-like voice. Talk to them like an adult. Don't raise your voice. Don't be mad. Don't show anger but talk to them firmly.

Give them a list of options and use logic to explain to them why they cannot have this cereal. That it's not good for them. That we can't afford it and that you're not going to buy it.

Then say "No."

Sometimes, especially the first time, they will start to cry. This is where you tell them that crying will not help. Crying will not change your mind. That they should not cry to try and get what they want. And that you will not give them what they want if they cry. Tell them that you know that they want the thing, whatever it is, but they cannot have it—no matter what.

This is not easy to do. It is hard to deal with your child crying in a semi-public place. The social pressure to conform is intense. But it is important to do it. It is important to talk to your children like adults—using calm, deep, unemotional language, with honest, concrete logic. It is important to let them know that you understand and feel their emotions but that logic trumps these emotions and they need to understand that there is a difference.

This is a perfect opportunity to begin to teach your child about choices. Tell them they have options. Teach them that they need to evaluate their options and make a decision. Talk to them about emotion and logic, and introduce these concepts into their mind at an early age.

Also, never, ever give in. Never break down and give them what they want. This will destroy whatever leverage you may have had. It takes many dozens of tries and times and examples of your lessons over many years of persistence, but it really helps your children wake up and learn how to be and how to think. And working on this lesson in the semi-public space like a grocery store is the perfect place to do this.

Also, this is another opportunity to teach your kids about the family.

Tell them that, no, they can't have that. That it's not good for them and it's not good for the family.

Talk to them about values. Explain to them that for now, their number one job is to be a better person and be a better big sister or little brother and think about the family. Tell them that they shouldn't be so selfish. Tell them that that box of Cap'n Crunch has too much sugar in it and that it's not good for them. Tell them that that is only something that they want, not something that they need. And tell them that it is time for them to grow up and start acting like a big girl, not a little baby (even when she is only three).

And then leave them there. Walk away. Walk away and continue with your shopping.

It was just a moment like this that happened to us when my daughter and I were shopping in a grocery store near our house. My daughter had found a box of cereal and was throwing a fit. I think she was three. She had thrown herself to the ground and was screaming and crying, pounding her fists on the floor. I had moved on. I hadn't reacted to her tantrum. I just calmly said no, put the box back on the shelf and continued with my shopping.

It was a while later when the manager of the grocery store found me several aisles away. I guess he felt that he needed to remind me of something. He approached and asked me, "Excuse me, sir, but is that your child screaming on aisle nine?"

I walked back to find my daughter all cried out sitting on the floor. I asked her if she was ready to go and she got up and came with me.

That was the last time that ever happened. Until, of course, my son came along. But by that time my daughter was old enough to explain to him the lesson.

Still, though, it took my son a little longer to cry it out.

But –

How do you build success into your kids?

How do you install systems of logic and reason into your children at an early age?

How do you teach your kids about self-reliance and personal responsibility?

How do you ignite their creative, inventive spark?

How can you teach your kids to play offense and attack?

How can you teach your kids to assert their freewill?

Superpower #11

Free Will

Do you believe in free will?

Is life determined? Has the story of our lives already been written, by either an all-seeing, all-powerful God or by the direct mechanical interplay between physical elements?

Or do you have free will? Do you have the power to change the future and control your destiny?

The subject of free will is complicated. Many people, among them hundreds of top scientists, believe that there is no free will. Or to use their language, free will is an illusion. They believe that if you believe in science and the scientific method, then you cannot believe in free will. They believe that if you start with the laws of physics and grind them all down to the foundations of our physical reality, there is no room for any kind of free will.

I used to think in these terms. I used to believe that humans had no free will. I spent the better part of a decade studying math and physics, engineering and cognitive science to try and understand my own mind and how it worked. For a while, I was seduced by the theory that there could be no free will. That humans do not have the capacity, mechanisms or ability to choose or to make a decision.

It took me a decade to learn the basics—to learn the things that you need to know to begin to understand the question. It takes about that much time just to read the work written by the major thinkers in the field. I mean, you have to start with the basics and work your way through it, but if you have the time and you are curious, it is a fabulous journey of understanding.

Anyway, if you take the time to grind your way through all of the prior art, down to the foundation of our known reality, you learn something very interesting. You learn that they don't know. They don't really know what's down there. I mean, they say they know. Scientists like to pretend that they understand the foundations of reality. But they really don't.

Maybe they're confused. Maybe they don't understand that the map is not the terrain. Maybe they are scared and they just want to believe in something. Maybe they hope that if they pretend like they know, they will be able to secure the next round of grant funding. But really, at the end of it all, they don't know what is really going on at the foundations of our physical reality.

If you take the time to drill down somewhere near the bottom of the pile, at the top of the first old, yellowed white paper, in the definitions of terms, they demand that you suspend belief and accept their definitions before you can evaluate their theory. You have to take a leap of faith. You have to accept the initial conditions of their simulation. You have to believe in their model. You have to have faith in their theory. You have to choose to believe in their model of reality before you begin to read their research.

So after 10 years of learning about this and thinking about this, I was asked to choose to believe in a model of reality in which there is no room for human choice.

Hmmm –

That seemed strange.

If their model leaves no room for human choice, how can I choose to accept their initial conditions?

This was too complicated. I was confused. I couldn't figure it out. At the time I was living on a boat, parked in dry dock, at Keehi Marine Center on Sand Island Road in Honolulu, Hawaii. I had been hired as crew to sail a multimillion-dollar racing yacht from Hawaii to San Diego, but we had broken the keel on a test lap around Maui, so we were stuck in dry dock with nothing much to do.

I was reading Moby Dick and obsessing over the conflicts between pre-determinism and free will. I was lonely and depressed and quite close to losing my mind.

I wanted to find some kind of objective baseline reality, and I had a lot of time on my hands, so I thought I would try something fun. I designed an experiment to run in my reality. Since I didn't accept their solution for the general case, I would try to derive a solution for my personal case.

Using myself as an n of one, I designed an experiment in which I was the test subject. I would live for a year believing and acting as if I had no free will. I would react only. I would only react. I would run on instinct and intuition. I wouldn't think about anything too much. I would pretend as if I had no free will. I would live as if my life story had already been written and there was no way to change the outcome. I would try to live as if my life's path had already been mapped out by some all-knowing deity and I couldn't do anything to change it. I would also try to think like that. I would try to control my thoughts by not dreaming of the future, planning things in advance or thinking about the past.

This thinking part turned out to be much harder to do. It is much harder to control your thoughts than it is to control your actions. But I decided to live like a determined automaton for one year. I figured that I had to give the system, the universe sufficient time to show measurable results for my experiment to be valid. And so I set down a small list of rules, kind of like commandments, guidelines that I could use to rule my life in some kind of deterministic way. The rules were pretty simple;

Rule #1 – Run on instinct
Don't plan, improvise. Don't dwell on the past; don't fantasize about the future. Why plan if your path is already drawn out on the map that has been carved by the wind and waves over millions of years?

Rule #2 – Set a routine
Do the same thing the same way every day. In your free time, distract yourself with trivial diversions.

Rule #3 - Never choose
If you have a decision to make, find a way to engage your fate. Do not weigh the options. Rely on a game of chance to make the choice. Flip a coin or roll the dice.

After a while, I fell into a groove and began to accept the daily routine, the moment by moment consciousness of a totally deterministic reality. I began to walk the path, the path that I assumed the all-knowing deity had drawn for me sometime shortly after the Big Bang.

This is a pleasant, blissful way to live. This "accept your fate" lifestyle removes all of the stress and worry of everyday life. It makes life easy and free. It throws you into the current of life where you are at the will of the universe.

Although this went against my intuitions, I felt like it was one way I might be able to find an objective truth for me. And since all objectivity originates with the individual as the prime source, I thought that this experiment might provide some kind of answer.

I decided to let my experiment run for one year. I figured that that would provide enough time to observe tangible results.

Well, that was an interesting three months.

What I learned was shocking. The evidence was overwhelming. My life fell apart. My life fell apart so fast that I had to curtail the experiment early.

Oh sure, life was easy and stress-free. You get to remove your personal responsibility and all of the hard work, stress and worry that decision-making takes, but my ability to make correct decisions disappeared.

Normally through the course of the days and weeks and months of a human life, one gets to make innumerable decisions. Most people in most places make bad decisions. They rely on fate.

Think about it. Think about all of the decisions that you have made in your life and all the decisions that you have seen your friends make in their lives. Give yourself a score. How many of those decisions did you make correctly? How many of these decisions did your friends make correctly? I would venture, speaking strictly for myself, that I have made maybe only 30% of my decisions correctly. The rest of my decisions were wrong. They were bad decisions. I should have chosen a different option. I didn't even break even. I didn't even score as good as random chance.

If I look at my friends, my peers in life that are roughly the same age, I can see that the really good, successful guys make only about 50% of their decisions well. I figure that if one could go through life making better decisions, they could raise their personal "correct decisions score." Doing this, they could create a massively more successful life.

So I began to ask myself: How could we improve our correct decision scores? How could we do things better?

There are basically two ways to make decisions. The first way is to use the fate method described above. The second way of making decisions would be using a kind of modern method to make the decision. This method goes something like this.

Step one -Define and prioritize your values.

Step Two -Choose your long-term goals based on your values.

Step Three -Compile a list of options based on facts.

Step Four -Gather information until a) your deadline is near or b) you have at least 70% of the information needed to make the decision.

Step Five -Weigh the positive and negative implications or reactions expected with each option based on logic.

Step Six -Choose the option that will provide the greater benefit to you based on your long-term goals.

This sounds obvious. It sounds so simple. You might be thinking, Duh, doesn't everybody do this? It is very simple, but the majority of people in the world do not use this method. They rely on fate. They flip the coin of destiny.

I learned three things from my experiment.

First, using the fate method you rarely do anything new. When you accept the confines of a determined automaton, you remove your creative impulse. You don't boldly go where no man has gone before. You just get in a rut and stay on the path. You don't invent or create anything; you just waste your life with mindless diversions. It is easy, simple and stress-free, but it is boring.

Second, the modern method takes a lot of work. If you believe in personal responsibility and you want to constantly strive to make your life better, you have to be "on" all the time. You have to be thinking and conscious all the time. You have to study and work every day. You have to be constantly gathering facts and evaluating options. You have to sweat and worry about each and every case, every decision. Implementing this modern method of decision-making takes a lot of work and introduces stress into every decision.

And third, I learned that this modern method of decision-making is a better way to make decisions. It gives you an actual step by step strategy that you can use to improve your overall decision score. When you use this modern method, your life will improve. It will improve slowly at first, but then as you improve your decision-making skills, the positive and correct decisions that you make will have a multiplying effect and your life will get better in an exponential way.

Because of this multiplying effect, I believe that this simple strategy is a powerful tool that you should teach your children while they are young.

To further clarify my point, I present here a cost/benefit analysis of fate versus free will.

In the costs column for the fate method:

Your life is unfulfilling. Oh sure, you can surf all day, dedicate your life to hedonistic play and meaningless diversions, but how long will that last? I guess that will depend on how smart you are. If you are simple, chasing happiness can last a lifetime. But if you are anywhere on the downward sloping side of the bell curve, happiness will get boring pretty quick. If you believe, like I do, that happiness comes from fulfillment and fulfillment comes from many years of hard work, then happiness without the fulfillment is unpleasant.

The other problem here is you don't get to accept the accolades. Let's say you believe in Fate and you find something that you love to do. You do that one thing. Let's say it is surfing. You surf every day for ten years and you get really, really good at surfing and you win a world championship. But wait; if you don't believe in free will, then you can't accept the trophy. You didn't have anything to do with your accomplishment. That was all written in the stars, or it was all God's will, or fate, or whatever. It wasn't you making the decision or working hard. It was just pure luck that got you to that point. A hedonistic life, unfulfilled.

In the benefits column for the fate method:

If you believe in fate, your life is carefree. Your life is easy. You don't have to worry about anything. Why worry? It can't change the outcome. You reject personal responsibility because you can't be responsible for something you can't control. If reality is determined either by supernatural forces or by physical interactions, you, as an operator, have no control, no choice, no action to take. That relieves you from any responsibility. Problem solved. All's you have to do is jump in the river of reality and let go. Let life take you wherever. Let your fate determine the outcome. Let Lady Luck guide your path. You will either be lucky or unlucky. The problem is the odds are not in your favor.

In the costs column for the modern method:

If you believe in free will, your life is hard. You have to take responsibility for everything that happens to you. Not just everything you do, but everything that happens in your life. Your fate is what you make. You have to think hard and work hard all the time. You have to worry and struggle and sweat over every decision and every choice. That is a lot of work. It is a 24/7/365 job.

In the benefits column for the modern method:

If you believe in free will, you have the largest possible chance to lead a fulfilling life. Let's say that you're in high school. You live near the beach and you love to surf. You decide that you want to become the world's greatest surfer. You examine the work schedule of the current pro surfers and you understand the dedication and time commitment associated with this goal. You make a list of the experiences in your life that you will have to sacrifice in order to obtain your objective. You make critical choices along the way. You blow off college. You blow off hanging with your friends. You don't drink. You don't smoke. You don't party. You get up every day a 4:00 AM to train. You invent a new surfboard that gives you an edge over the other competitors. And you work hard, every day, for ten years. By the time you are 26 years old, you win the world championship. You step up to this podium in a different way. You know how hard you have worked. You know the sacrifices that you have made to take that last step. It was your hard work, sacrifice, innovation, and dedication that brought you to this point in your life. It was all you. This is a meaningful life. This is a life fulfilled.

And how does this play out?

It's time to level up –

Imagine that we multiply this concept by 100 million.

How would this strategy change our community and our society? What would be the ripple effect?

Imagine if we teach this system to every 3-year-old child in the world. What impact would it have?

Each child would begin by mimicking their parents. They would slowly learn how to implement this strategy at an early age, defining and redefining their values. Each child will begin to dream of different possible goals and what their life might look like. Each child will begin to explore different versions of their possible future. Each child would begin to direct their energies towards specifically defined goals.

Instead of people stumbling through life, letting events randomly unfold haphazardly in front of them, they could, from an early age, lead directed lives pursuing defined goals in accordance with known values.

We could be living in a world of focused, driven people that are actively pursuing a positive, optimistic future.

The world is messed up. There are a lot of problems to be solved. We will need to leverage our creative strengths, combine our talents, ignite our passions and invent our way into the future.

We are going to need a legion of strong, virile, competent, creative, freedom-loving superheroes.

We are going to have to raise kids that reject the carefree life and embrace the worry, sweat and struggle of a life with choice. We are going to have to raise kids that know how to make choices.

Kids that are strong enough and confident enough to face the unknown and enjoy moving through an indeterminate future.

We need to raise badass kids that know that they can create and innovate their way through any catastrophe.

We will need a bunch of kids that want to play offense, that want to attack.

They want to create.

They want to invent.

They want to solve problems.

We want to raise our kids to be comfortable with uncertainty.

We want our kids to be strong and embrace the suffering.

We want our kids to embrace the suffering of independence and self-reliance.

We want our kids to embrace the challenges of freedom.

Because those are the kids—the kids that know how to act, the kids that know how to play offense—that are going to be able to create the future that we, as a species, are going to want to live in.

Commit yourself to becoming a Superdaddy and raise Superhero Kids.

Section 3

WHAT'S THE POINT?

Why are we doing this? Why are we living our lives? Why are we going to school and going to work? Why are we getting married and having kids?

What's the point? What's the purpose?

We are kind of all taught now that there is no point.

We are kind of taught now that there is no God and life has no meaning.

We are taught that we are each a small, insignificant speck of dust in the interstellar wind and that it doesn't matter what you do or how hard you struggle, your life will come and go and no one will care.

You, as a simple, mild-mannered man, don't have the power or ability to change anything.

Most people in the modern Western world have been taught these three strange tales:

1. The Earth is already scarred. We have burned too much carbon, and global warming will soon overheat the planet and kill us all.

2. The carrying capacity of the Earth has been overextended for decades. There are already too many people on the planet, and we will soon use up all of the natural resources and die of famine.

3. We as a species have produced too much rubbish, and we will soon all drown in a planetary toilet of rotting sewage.

With an outlook on life this bleak, why would anyone ever try to do something important?

It's too late. It's already over. Why even try? Why go on?

Why don't we just party our brains out and have a good time? Why don't we just lead the hedonistic life? Why don't we just throw our own little drug-induced, 24-hour, raging rave orgy?

Why should we waste time doing anything important? Why don't we just party until the music stops?

Some people say that the one thing that you can do to save the world is to not have any kids. They say this because they believe in the 200-year-old theory of the Malthusian Catastrophe. They believe that human life is the true evil and that the problem of human overpopulation is driving all of the other problems on the planet. They believe that there are already too many people that burn too much carbon, eat too much food, consume too much, and make too much garbage. They also believe that you having children will make the problems of overpopulation, climate change, starvation, materialism, and pollution worse.

I know many couples that have fallen into this trap. They didn't have kids because they had been taught that there were already too many people on the planet, and they wanted to help save the planet by not having any kids.

Hell, I even fell into that trap. I stopped having kids after I had two kids partly because I wanted to do my part. I wanted to help save the planet as I knew it.

So, in the middle of my prime breeding years, I had an operation to permanently stop my very own personal population bomb. If I had known then what I know now, I would have started earlier and I would have had more children.

If you think about life on Earth as a problem and you think about all of the other problems that spiral out of that problem, it can quickly become overwhelming. And if you think about these problems long enough and hard enough, for 20 years or so, they quickly boil down to these three basic questions:

1. What's the point?
2. Why are we here?
3. What is the meaning of life?

Well, I have put my 10,000 hours into these questions and I have an answer.

Why should we do this? We should do this because of Isaac Newton and his second law.

The Second Law and Human Life

The purpose of human life in four steps

Life

Life is really very strange. Life emerged over millions and millions of years on Earth. Nobody knows why life arose out of the primordial ooze, and I'm not sure we will ever know for sure how life arose out of the vat of stagnant pond scum that might have been there near the beginning of life. But if you think about it from a product development point of view, life is the most expensive and valuable product that has ever come into being. It has taken more time, more energy, more work, more testing and more luck to create than anything else in the universe.

To get life, one would have to have a bunch of different elements sitting in the pond. These elements had to be forged in a supernova blast somewhere nearby before our own sun was born. That star had to burn for billions of years, die, explode and blast heavier elements into space. Then after millions of years, these elements were pulled together by gravity to form our sun and our solar system.

There had to be just the right amount of elements in just the right proportions. They had to be formed into a planet of just the right size just far enough away from the sun where there could be liquid water. Then this liquid water had to sit around in a stagnant pond for millions of years until, for some unknown reason, some random combination of elements bumped together in just the right way to form a cell or something. Then this something had to lie around for millions of years while the earth was cooling and the atmosphere was changing into just the right percentages of nitrogen, oxygen, and other elements to make more life possible. Then after more millions of years, this something had to accidentally bump into other goo in just the right way for the next strange step in the evolutionary chain to occur.

147

This went on for billions of years, in just the right ways, at just the right times for life to happen on our planet Earth. I'm going to go way out on a limb here and go against the common theory and say that there is no other intelligent life in the universe. We are the only ones here.

Even if there are billions and billions of other Earth-like planets in our galaxy, the odds are just too high that there was just the right stuff in just the right proportions at just the right time on just the right planet just far enough from the sun to recreate just the right life to make a self-aware lifeform. Now there might be something outside of our galaxy, but if that is the case, they are just too effen far away to make any difference.

So we're the only ones here. There's nobody else. No other intelligent life in our galaxy or in the universe or anywhere else for that matter. We're it.

And if you think about life, intelligent life, from a product development point of view, the human brain is the most expensive, most valuable thing in the universe. Because the human brain can change the future.

Energy

What is energy? Energy comes in many forms—potential, kinetic, mechanical, heat and more. It is important to remember that energy cannot be created or destroyed and that all the energy that is bouncing around the universe now has always been there and will always be there.

We are incredibly lucky to live on a planet that has a net-positive supply of energy. The sun beats down on our Earth, showering us with a little bit of extra energy every day. Some of this energy bounces off and goes back into space. Some of the energy gets redirected and repurposed into plants and other living things. Some of the energy is used to run the thermal weather system that makes rain and redistributes heat. It is this little bit of extra energy that makes life possible on this planet. Life is really just another way of evenly distributing this little bit of extra energy around the planet.

Life has "learned" how to repurpose these different forms of energy to make more life. Human life has learned to redirect and repurpose energy to make almost anything. The most exciting, thrilling and satisfying activity that any human can do in life is to redirect energy. And the more energy that you can redirect, the more exciting it is.

Think about it. Anytime you can direct energy, you are having fun. And the more energy that you get to direct, the more fun you will have. When you ski down a mountain, you are redirecting the potential energy that you stored up when you took the chairlift to the top. When you do any kind of motorsports, be it driving a car, racing a motorcycle, flying a plane, riding a snowmobile, or piloting anything with an engine, you are purposely redirecting energy from some kind of hydrocarbon dug out of the Earth's crust. If you run or play any sport, you are redirecting the sun's energy that had been stored up in a plant, was eaten and then reused in the mussels in your legs. The most exciting, most exhilarating and most fun thing a human can do is redirect energy, and the more energy that you can control, the more fun you will have.

Humans are the only thing in the known universe that can redirect energy with purpose. Oh sure, a plant can redirect energy and make another plant, and an animal can redirect energy, react to a predator and run away. But a human is the only thing in the known universe that can think of a thing, build a contraption, and make a system that he dreams up that purposely redirects energy into anything he wants. The human mind is the only thing in the universe that can change the future. The human mind can actively, proactively build a building, plan a city, reform entire continents in forms that only he has imagined by using energy the way he sees fit.

So energy is the most important thing in the universe. And the control of and the redirection of energy is the human being's highest purpose.

The Second Law of Thermodynamics

All of these fundamental questions go back to, rely upon, and are fundamental to Newton's second law of thermodynamics. The second law of thermodynamics states that in a natural thermodynamic process, there is an increase in the sum of the entropies of the participating systems. To state this in simple terms, what the second law says is that everything all the time slows down, gets cold and goes gray. Everything is driven towards an increasing state of homogeny. Everything all the time is turning into a kind of lukewarm, completely homogenized, gray mayonnaise. All energies disperse. Everything hot cools down. Everything rots. Everything decays. Everything rusts and falls away, everything, all the time. That's a LAW.

Everything, that is, except one thing.

There is only one thing in the universe that fights against the second law.

And that one thing is life.

When examined over a limited time span, life is the only thing in the universe that can control and redirect energy. Life can take energy, collect energy, and repurpose energy, or refocus energy to its purpose. A plant can passively collect the energy of sunlight and repurpose, redirect and refocus this energy towards its own personal, selfish goal of projecting its DNA. A plant can make a flower, build a seed and project its own personal genetic code, its prodigy, a mirror image of itself into the future.

Life is the only thing that can do that. The only thing in the known universe that can go against the second law of thermodynamics is life. Without life, the universe is on a one-way path, an out of control train, a sun-diving descent to hell. And hell, in this case, is the medium-cold, kind of gray, totally equally distributed sewer of the end of times.

The human mind is the only thing in the known universe that can counter, fight against and stop the most powerful evil force in the universe, entropy.

The human mind is the only thing in the known universe that can redirect and repurpose energy in such a way that we can literally conceive, design and build our future world.

The human mind is the only thing in the universe that can fight and reverse the second law of thermodynamics.

And the human mind, the most valuable and expensive thing ever created, is the only thing that can purposely redirect energy to its own ends, preserving the human mind, the most valuable and expensive thing in the universe.

The Meaning of Life

So what does this have to do with you, your life and your ability to do something of meaning?

- *Because Sex* -

You hold in your body the ability to make a life. You hold in your hands the power to create the only thing in the known universe that can go against the second law. You can make a child. You can make a copy of yourself.

And because of life, because of energy, because of the second law, making more life is the purpose of life. Making more life brings life meaning. One might ask: Why are we here? What is our purpose?

We are here to use the most expensive and valuable thing in the universe, our human brain, to redirect energy to counter the second law and make more life. That is our purpose. That is our meaning. That is why we are here.

We are here to make more life, to make more human brains—human brains that will invent new ways to redirect energy and counter the second law.

We need to work together

to save the human mind

from entropy, the evilest force in the universe.

151

Most siblings in most families fight with each other all of the time.

It is very rare for brothers and sisters to grow up together loving each other as friends and teammates.

Would you like to be able to give your kids one of the most powerful gifts in the world?

Would you like to give your children the gift of friendship and comradery?

LESSON TWELVE

How to keep your children from fighting with each other

Sibling rivalry is a serious thing, and it messes up a lot of families. For some reason, your kids instinctively want to bully, brutalize and dominate each other. How do you keep that from happening? And how do you keep these vicious, brutal, physical fights from destroying your children and their relationships with each other later in life?

There is a natural Darwinian trait amongst mammalian offspring in tight-knit families to compete. This is perfectly natural. It happens in every young family of almost every animal species on the planet. It happens in every bird's nest, in every bear den, every bat cave and every gorilla hollow where there are two close siblings vying for the parents' attention. It is perfectly natural and it happens for a reason.

Somewhere programmed into the wetware of every animal on the planet, there is a secret module of code. This is the Secret Code of Understanding. This secret code is like the boot program on your computer. It is the first thing that turns on in the human animal and every other animal on the planet. This code starts all the other systems running. It tells the heart how to pump, the lungs how to breathe and the brain how to boot up.

It is the code that tells the baby giraffe how to stand up, the baby trout how to point its nose upstream and the baby human how to find its mother's milk.

This code is poorly understood by humans because it is hidden from our conscious mind. This program is running underneath our mind in a secret part of our brain that we can't see. It is running in the background, and we have very little understanding of what it does, how it works or what the original instructions are.

Part of this secret code runs the biological systems of our bodies like how to digest food, how to pump blood and how to breathe. Part of the code gives us critical information about how the world and the universe works. It's really kind of crazy when you think about it that somewhere in everyone's head there is embedded a secret set of basic rules about how the universe works that we don't even know about. Some of these rules are about gravity and some of these rules are about light. These rules might say things like "don't piss into the wind" or "don't get too close to the edge of a cliff." Some of these rules are about love and romance, and some of these rules are about your personal relationships. These rules might manifest in strange ways like the kind of sick feeling you get when your best friend's girlfriend starts flirting with you. We are running this simple subroutine all the time, every day and everywhere we go.

One of the rules running within this super-secret subroutine gives every human infant some deep, intuitive knowledge about how to survive in the crib or cave or wherever he is. And I'm guessing that one of the rules goes something like this.

"Your parents have limited resources. They only have so much food. They only have a certain amount of time. They only can give you a few moments of attention. They only have a specific amount of emotional energy, and they only have a very limited amount of love that they can spend on you each day."

This is law. This is fact. This is hard written into every animal on the planet. Babies instinctively know this and react accordingly. Every baby in every nest understands this basic idea and knows that if it wants to survive and thrive, it has to compete with the other siblings in its nest for the time, attention, energy and love of its mother and father. The winner of this competition gets more food, more energy and more support than the other kids in the nest. And with these additional resources, the winner gets bigger and stronger and faster and smarter. And with that, the winner kids will be more able to compete with all of the other kids in all the other nests.

As you can imagine, if one of your kids is already a little bit bigger and a little bit stronger than the other kids, he is going to beat up the other kids so that he can become the winner kid in his nest. He will do this automatically, he will do this instinctively, he will do this all the time every day, and he will do this without knowing why he's doing it or that it might be wrong.

There are very few ways that we as the human overlords of our own mind can rewrite this secret code, but just as you can go in and program the boot code of your laptop, we can go in and change a few things in our secret code.

This is one of the modules of code that needs to be rewritten. As a parent, you need to rewrite this code in your kids so that at the very least you can maintain a healthy balance of sanity in your home. But, even more importantly, you need to rewrite this code so that you can give your children one of the most important gifts of their lifetime—the gift of having their brother or sister as their very best friends.

If you can rewrite this code, you can turn your kids from brutal competitors to synergistic teammates.

If you can rewrite this code, you can raise your kids so that as they grow they build long-term, healthy relationships and become each other's best friends.

So next let's talk about how to rewrite the boot code of your kids.

LESSON THIRTEEN

Get their buy-in

So how do you keep your kids from fighting with each other?

First of all, it's important to understand that you will have better results if you start early. That doesn't mean you can't start now, but it does mean that the sooner you start, the better results you'll have.

How soon should you start?

Hmmm –

To tell you the truth, we started three years before our second kid was born.

My mother once told me, "Never have kids two years apart. You either have to have your two kids one right after the other or wait until the first kid is three before you have your second kid. You don't want to have your second kid come along while your first kid is going through his Terrible Twos. This makes your kids want to kill each other."

I took this rule to heart and we waited a while between having our first kid and our second kid. So, first of all, if you can, wait two years after having a baby before you start thinking about having another baby. So that way the second baby comes along after your first baby's third birthday.

Next thing, when you just have one kid, and you know you want to have more than one, talk to your first kid about having a baby brother or baby sister. Ask your kid, "Do you want to have a baby brother? Are you going to be nice to your baby brother? Are you going to help out with raising our baby?" This starts your first kid thinking about having another kid in the house, and it helps with the transition later.

Next, before the second kid is born, you'll need to get your first kid's buy-in.

A "buy-in" is a business sales strategy that uses emotions and ego to entice your customer into buying your product. With this strategy, you give your customer a creative chore to do as part of the product.

Years ago, I was living as an illegal alien in Stockholm, Sweden. As an illegal alien, I had all of the rights and privileges that most illegal aliens have. Illegal aliens have no rights. Since I had no rights, I couldn't get a work permit. And since I couldn't get a work permit, I couldn't get a job. So since I couldn't have a real job, I did all of the things that all IA's do all over the world. I picked produce. I went door-to-door delivering political flyers, and I worked in sweatshops.

At this one particular sweatshop, I worked for an aging Swedish supermodel. She was trying to start her own brand of clothes. What she did was brilliant. She would go around to every little expensive boutique in Sweden and ask to have coffee with the owner. Since everyone knew who she was and because she was beautiful, everyone always said yes. Then she would meet with the owner and tell her what she was trying to do. She told them that she loved designing clothes and asked if she could design an outfit for the owner. She would whip out her sketch pad and start drawing. She would tell the owner to stand up and turn around while she sketched out her image. Then she would say, "What is your dream outfit? How do you want this to look?" Then they would have a couple glasses of wine and she would sketch away. She would pull out a big book of sample materials and let the owner pick the colors and the fabrics. By the end of the lunch, she would have drawings and patterns for the owner's dream outfit. Then she would say to the owner, "Oh my God, oh my God, this is brilliant. This is fabulous. We should make this outfit and sell it in your shop. I'll bet that you sell a million of these."

Ultimately what she was doing was fulfilling the owner's fantasies of being a famous fashion designer. She was also getting the owner's buy-in.

Then she would start The Close. "How many outfits do you want to order?" The owner now had her ego involved. If she said one, the owner didn't trust her own instincts, and she couldn't do that in front of the beautiful Swedish supermodel. No, she had to order 100 sets of outfits in different sizes and in different colors. This is a very successful sales strategy.

Back to my point, to get someone's buy-in, you give them some fun thing to do, usually, some creative aspect of the project to do that will influence the final product. This way the stakeholder that does his creative thing will want to show that his creative thing was cool. If the project is a success, then his part was cool. So he wants the project to be a success to prove that his creative thing worked and the project was cool. And oh, by the way, for the project to be a success, he has to buy the product.

So try to find a way to get your first kid's buy-in on this baby project before the baby comes along. Ask the first kid for help getting the house ready and making a great space for the second kid. Make a nice bed or a new bedroom. Have him or her help pick out the colors and materials. Let the first kid pick out clothes and toys to give to the baby after the baby is born. This way the first kid will want to see the successful influence of their creative endeavor. The first kid will want to see the second kid thrive.

One of the things that we did with our daughter to get her buy-in was to ask our three year old to help us name the baby. We told our daughter that we were going to have another kid and we said we needed her help. We wanted her to help us raise the baby and take care of it. We also told her that we needed help with a name.

So after we knew for sure that my wife was pregnant and we were really going to have another baby, I went to our daughter and told her the story. I told her that there was a baby growing inside Mommy's tummy and that she was going to be a big sister. I told her that we were going to need help with the baby and that we were going to make a big list of chores and jobs and responsibilities for her. Our daughter, mind you, was three and this made her very excited. She was excited to have chores and jobs and responsibilities. She couldn't wait. She was just that kind of kid.

And then I told her that we needed help with a name. I said that we wanted her to pick a middle name for the baby. She just stopped in her tracks and looked at me with wide eyes. She touched her fingertips to her lips and said, "Oh my gosh, oh my gosh, oh my gosh, I have it, I have it." She raised her arms in the air and said, "I have the perfect name." She spread her arms apart as if unfurling a banner and said,

TREE AVENUE

Isn't that the most beautiful name?

Tree Avenue

I told her that it was a pretty name, but it wasn't quite right for this. We needed a name for a little boy. She said, "Ok, how about, hmmm, how about...

THUNDER

I said that was perfect.

So now our son's middle name is Thunder. It actually turns out to be a very good name for him.

This is a simple example, just one way that you can reach out to your firstborn and get their buy-in, their help, and understanding that they are going to be part of the process. That they are going to have jobs and responsibilities. This kind of thing helps switch their mindset from competitor to teammate. This lets them know and gives them time to reframe their ideas about their position in the family. It gives them the chance to change their role from only-child to big-sister.

And here is what you want. You want your firstborn to own the process. You want your first kid's ego involved in the success of the second kid. You want the first kid to do everything they can to help the second kid thrive. You want both your kids to understand that they are on a family team and for the team to win, each member of the team has to be great.

If you can do this, you will go a long way towards rewriting the boot code of your kids' minds. And if you can do that, you will set your kids up to be the very best of friends throughout their entire lives.

But how do you do that? What real steps can you take to rewrite their code and help you kids treat each other with respect and empathy?

LESSON FOURTEEN

The Family Game

Okay, so now the other baby has come along and you have this new thing in the house. The whole social dynamic gets knocked out of balance. Your sleep patterns have to change, your daily routines have to change, and you pretty much have to reinvent entirely new ways of living your life.

It is always really fun to have a new baby in the house, and I'm sure our house was a lot like millions of other people's houses. We were really lucky. My wife had finagled a deal at work where she could stay home for a while after the baby came. So, for a while there, we all got to stay home and play with the baby.

Of course, not everybody was happy about that. Our daughter wasn't used to not being the center of attention, but she was getting on pretty well. The biggest shock was our cat. At the time we had this really badass cat. He was an alley find that we had adopted off the street. Our daughter had found him as a little baby kitten in the gutter one day. Someone had poured lighter fluid all over him and lit him on fire. He was burned pretty badly, and a lot of his hair was gone. We had nursed him back to health, and he decided to stick around. We called him Frizzle.

This little kitten grew up to be one of the biggest, baddest-ass cats I had ever known. He could catch a hummingbird in midair, and he was always bringing us headless lizards or half dead rats to show us his appreciation. He would leave these "gifts" on our doorstep or in our bed.

Well, when we brought our son into our house, Frizzle wasn't having it. The baby was taking up his space and he wasn't happy. We couldn't leave the baby on the floor because the cat would hiss and bat at it. And one time I left the baby on the bed to take a nap. I turned around and walked away, and I heard what I thought were muffled cries coming from the bed. I ran over there to find our cat straddling the baby's face. I think he was trying to smother our son. The cat looked up at me as if to say, "Just give me a couple more minutes and I'll take care of this problem for you."

Needless to say, that was the last time the cat came into the house for a while. As it turns out, our daughter was doing great, but I had forgotten to get buy-in from our cat.

So, what's the next thing? What can you do next?

The next thing you want to do is you want to build a team. And to get your kids to play like a team, you have to give them a game.

So here's the game you give your kids to play.

You tell your kids that there is a Game. This Game is going on all around you right now. All the other families are playing the Game and they are playing against each other. The Game goes on all day and all night, 24 hours a day, seven days a week and every day of the year. Even on Christmas Day.

The object of this Game is to see which family is the strongest family. To win the Game, each person in the family has to show that they have the best mommy, the best daddy and the best sister of all of the other families around. And your sister or brother; your mother and father also have to show that they have the best sisters and brothers and mothers and fathers around.

And to do that you have to be the best little brother or big sister you can be. That way your mother and father and your sister or brother knows that you are the best and can prove it by your actions.

This is a secret game. And it is a little bit like the Fight Club. The first rule of the Fight Club is: don't talk about the Fight Club. Nobody talks about it, even though everybody is playing the Game. Nobody ever talks about it. They keep it a secret. They play the Game. They keep score and later in life, after your kids have grown up and started their own families, everybody makes sure that you know what families have won and what families have lost.

So now that you've told them the basic rules of the Game, you have different instructions for each of the siblings. If you have an older boy and a younger girl, you can switch up the instructions to match. If you have two boys or two girls, you might need to change the instructions. Anyway, I'm going to give you these different instruction sets and you can mix and match as you go.

For the older daughter:

You tell your daughter that it is her number one job to help her little brother grow up to be bigger, better, faster, stronger and smarter than SHE is. She wants to do this because all of the other families know that if the little brother wins the Game, the whole family wins the Game.

You tell her that she is the first player through the Game and that she has to learn all of the tricks and tips and pass these tips on to her brother. Tell her that she might make a wrong move once in a while, but even these mistakes are very valuable. It will be important to the family to remember that mistake and pass that information along to her little brother so that he doesn't waste time making the same mistake. It is her job to learn everything that she needs to know to be a good big sister and then pass these secrets, this information on to her little brother.

It is also her job to care for and take care of her little brother. It is a big job taking care of a baby, and we will need her help.

Also, it is important to remember that the object of the Game is to win the Game. And to win the Game she has to help the whole family win the Game.

So it is her job to work as hard as she can, study as hard as she can, learn everything that she needs to know to be a really good person, and then pass that information on to her little brother so that he can be a really good person. It is her job to make her little brother even better than she is.

You tell her that she wants to do this because the object of the Game is to make a really good family.

You will need to remind your daughter from time to time that it is not her job to discipline her little brother or tell him what to do. That is her parents' job. If she ever hits her little brother or hurts her little brother in any way, her mom and dad will be very disappointed in her and she will lose their trust.

You will need to tell them that if either one of them ever hits or hurts their brother or sister in any way, that will be doing something very wrong. They will be making the family weak. If they do something like that, they will make the daddy look like a bad daddy and the mommy look like a bad mommy. They will be bringing shame on the family and they will look like a bad sister or brother. They will be going against the rules of the Game and going against their own fundamental purpose.

So, if you are to fight with your brother, hit him or hurt him in any way, you are going against your most fundamental purpose.

This is what you tell your older daughter. And here is what you tell your younger son.

Tell your son that the dad is the man of the family. It is the job of the man of the family to take care of and protect the family. If someone were to mess with you or your mother or your sister, it is the number one job of the dad to go out there and mess them up. It is the job of the dad to protect his wife and his kids.

Then you tell him that when the dad isn't around he, the son, becomes the man of the family. So, when the dad isn't around, it becomes the son's job to be the man of the family. And as the man of the family, it will be the son's job to protect your mother and your sister.

So, if you fight with your sister or hit her or hurt her in any way, you will be going against your number one job, your fundamental purpose.

Your fundamental purpose is to become a really good little brother and a really good person. Your job is to become the best person you can be and the best player you can be on the family team. Your fundamental purpose is to help the family win the Game. And you will help the family win the Game by becoming the best team player you can be and the best person you can be.

So you will need to work hard and study hard. You will need to learn everything that you need to learn to be a good person and then pass that information up to your sister so that she can be a better team player and a better person.

Once you set these rules down and start the Game in play, you will notice that your kids will want to play the Game. If things get out of hand and they start to fight, you remind them that the Game is on and that they are going against their fundamental purpose.

You will be amazed at how well this works. You may need to remind your kids of the rules and help your kids refocus on the bigger picture, but little kids want to do one thing more than anything else in the world; they want to be bigger. They want to be older. They want to seem like big kids, teenagers or adults. When you dangle an opportunity for them to be bigger, they will usually jump at it.

So if they are fighting or emotional or in a rage, pull them aside for a moment, hold them for a while, love them up, calm them down and tell them about the Game again. Remind them of the rules and tell them that's it's time for them to grow up and start playing the Game.

They will quiet down and start to play the Game. They will stop fighting and get back to work.

You will not believe how well this works.

And when it works, you will have given them, the brother and the sister, one of the most precious things in the whole human world. You will give them the chance to have their brother or their sister as their very best friend.

You can be one of the few families in which the brothers and sisters grow up together loving each other as friends and teammates.

You can give your kids one of the most powerful gifts in the world.

You can give your children the gift of friendship and comradery.

You can provide your children a family where they grow up with their brother or sister as their very best friend.

Teach your kids to play the Family Game.

Superpower #14

Super Friends

It is hard to get your kids to go against their natural instincts. It takes a lot of effort, attention, and persistence to catch, refocus and train your kids. As a Superdaddy you will become like a mega-ninja Bonsai gardener, gently molding and forming your kids, guiding them toward a more positive light.

When your kids grow up to be allies instead of adversaries, they multiply their strengths and advantages.

If they undercut each other as rivals, they degrade and diminish each other's foundations. And as they grow through their early influential childhood, this degradation can have a massively negative multiplying effect. It degrades their sense of self, their sense of their abilities and their optimism.

But...

When they support each other as teammates, all of these attributes turn 180 degrees. Each of your kids becomes more confident and secure. Each of your kids becomes more calm and compassionate.

And these attributes also have a massively positive multiplying effect. Your kids grow up to be bigger and stronger, healthier and more active.

Every year that your children spend being supported and encouraged by their sibling, they move up a level in cognitive, social and physical abilities, and—like with compound interest—these attributes grow stronger with a multiplying effect. They not only get the benefit from their growth, but they get the benefit compounded from the growth they experienced from the year before and the year before that.

But that's not all –

The most important thing that happens when you build a team within your family is the bond your children will make among themselves.

Developing the strong bond of friendship between siblings is a friendship like no other. It is more fundamental, more foundational, more influential. It lasts longer and is more significant than any other relationship that you will build.

Having your brother or sister as your best friend is the most powerful friendship that one can build.

And having your children become best friends is an immensely fulfilling, gratifying and satisfying accomplishment.

If you are successful at building a team to play the Family Game and your children grow up to become best friends, your kids will love you for it and love you forever.

What is the meaning of life?

Why are we here?

Do you want your life to have meaning?

Do you want to know your greater purpose?

Do you want to connect to something bigger than

just yourself and your life?

LESSON FIFTEEN

DNA vs. RNA

So this is part of the strategy. The strategy is that you want to pull your kids out of the smaller, ego-centric view of themselves and into a larger, family-oriented view. You want to give your kids, from the earliest possible time, the idea that they are part of a bigger plan—that there is a plan, that you have a plan, and that they are part of this plan.

You want to tell your kids a story. You want to tell your kids the story of their life. You want to tell your kids the story of their lives in the context of the family. You want to tell your kids the story of your family both the past and the future. And you want to place your kids in that story so that they start to understand that they are part of a bigger thing, a bigger picture. They are part of a family, and this family is a big deal.

Now if you don't know the story—if you don't know the story of your family, your own past, your story—then you need to find that out. You need to learn the story of your own family. This is a crucial, critical step in the process of becoming fully human.

Every major religion in the world is a story about a family. Every religion in the world provides truths and lessons and advice, and all of this information is wrapped around and consolidated into and told through a story. And that story is the story of a family. Where it started, where it is and where it's going.

Some religions, as part of a coming-of-age narrative, compel their children to research their family. They make them plot their family's history back through time to understand who came before them and learn what their ancestors went through. This lesson isn't just an exercise in genealogy and dogma. It is a way to place your child into the bigger picture. It is a way to give your children the weight and responsibility of a bigger life, a greater purpose. It is a way to give your kids meaning and purpose in life.

The purpose of this exercise is to wrap your children into the fabric of life. You want to show them that they have commitments and obligations to their past and their future. You need to tell them the story.

And the story goes something like this –

You have an obligation to your past.

You are part of this family. You have many, many ancestors, fathers, and mothers, grandfathers and grandmothers, great-grandfathers and great-grandmothers that have come before you. These were great people that did sometimes unbelievably difficult and dangerous things. They took on heroic, Herculean tasks and did work on things that you can hardly comprehend. You have an obligation to these ancestors to continue in this great tradition. You don't want to embarrass or tarnish the reputation of your ancestors. You want to make them proud. You want to impress them. You want to build the respect, ethos, credibility, and cache of the family name. You want to build brand value in the name brand, in YOUR NAME BRAND.

You need to step up and take your place amongst the heroes that came before you. You need to be able to stand beside the visions of your great-great-great grandfather and have him be proud to be standing next to you.

That is the history of your family—that is the DNA. That is kind of like making a map of the transfers of DNA from generation to generation. That is the past.

You also need to talk about the future of the family and talk about where they are going and what influence they will have, the guidance they will have on the future of the family.

To do this, it is good to understand a little bit about Ribonucleic Acid (RNA).

Some RNA molecules play an active role within cells by catalyzing biological reactions, controlling gene expression, or sensing and communicating responses to cellular signals.

RNA can turn your genes on and off, and what we are learning about epigenetics right now is truly astounding. DNA may be the blueprint of life, but RNA can hide parts of the blueprint so that it never gets built, or it can turn on older, hidden parts of your DNA that were not turned on when you were made.

In other words, there is a way that you can actually make a better kid. There is a way that you can physically change the expression of your DNA in your child to be bigger, stronger, smarter, faster and better than you are. The scary part is—there are also ways that you can build a kid that expresses the worst parts of you and makes a kid that has all of the things that you hate about yourself.

From the father, this epigenetic process might happen at the moment of conception. So, the person that you are, the man that you are, the place that you are in life at the time you mate with your wife is the person your baby is going to be when he grows up.

Think about that for a moment. What you eat and what you drink, what you think and how you feel, even the simple diversions that consume your awareness might be passed down to your kids.

I believe that this works in all kinds of funny and fabulous ways.

For instance, this probably works in the physical space, like what you eat and what you drink. So, if you are eating healthy foods and working out every day, your baby will grow up to like healthy foods and love to stay in shape.

This could also work on a cognitive level. So, let's say that in the period of your life that you are mating with your wife, you are working on a huge, mentally challenging, technical problem. If what we know about epigenetics is true, your baby will grow up with a bigger brain and your kid will be smarter than you.

This could also work on an emotional level. I believe that your kids, the kids that you have, actually channel your emotional state. They actually grow up expressing the same general vibe that you were in when you mated with your partner. If you are in a high point in your life, if you had just achieved a huge success or were riding a wave of winning, if all the lights were green for you that day or that week and everything was going well when you were working on having a child, then they will be a happy, successful, winning kid.

This could also work on crazy things like the type of music you like, the type of clothes or shoes that you were wearing at the time, the kind of house you were living in and the type of car you were driving.

So RNA turns on and off your genes. And these genes build the baby that will be growing in your partner. This mechanism channels a version of you into the baby. The epigenetic mechanism builds like a snapshot, an image, a freeze frame of you at the time of your mating and passes it through to your baby. This includes everything like what you eat and how you physically move. It includes the habits you do every day and how you walk and talk. It also may include the way you think and what you think about. It even might include your view of life, your politics and your attitudes towards current events.

But that is not all; this snapshot also includes things you can't even quantify. It includes things like shape and style and tastes and vibe that you never think about and don't know that you even notice.

Now, I know that the father only gets one-half of the influence. I know that each child gets one-half of the mommy's genes and one-half of the daddy's genes. So, the same snapshot goes in at the same time from the momma. And if the momma is working out every day or working on a really challenging problem or having a massive success at work or whatever she's doing, those genes will be expressed in the baby as well.

To me, it is no wonder why our daughter is so effen smart. Some people wonder: How could we—how could I, simple-minded as I am—have such an incredibly bright baby child? How could I have had a kid with such a big brain? Well, it's no mystery to me. If I think back at the time of her conception, what were we doing? My wife was working on her Ph.D. at UCLA. She was working her brain as hard as she could for as long as she could every day. And I had a full-time job working all day and then staying up half the night designing a new invention. I was using my creative mind as hard as I could all day long and half the night to think up new ideas. Our situation is just one antidotal story, but if what we are learning about epigenetics is true, it would explain a lot about how my kids have turned out.

Now let's get to the scary part. Let's get back to you and your family. Your family's past and your family's future. Here it comes. Here comes the scary part. This idea gives you a snapshot of how you can really mess this up.

If you think about how powerful this is, if you understand how RNA works and what it does, if you get the idea that a snapshot of your life will be passed down to the next generation, and the one after that and the one after that, if you start to get the idea that you now hold—right now, today, in this instant—the future of the genome of your family from here on into all-time eternal, you begin to realize that how you are now and what you are doing will change the destiny of everything and everyone that comes after you.

You will know that if you're a drunk right now, your kids will probably be drunks. If you're wasting your life getting stoned and playing video games, your kids will grow up to want to just get stoned and screw off all day. If you eat bad food and don't work out and stay inside and mope on the couch, your kids, and their kids and their kids are going to be doing the same stupid stuff for the rest of their lives.

So you know that you could change your bad behaviors now. Or, you could leave this difficult chore of changing behaviors to your kids to struggle with. Wouldn't it be better if you did the heavy lifting now so that your kids and their kids and their kids will have better lives?

Make a commitment now to change the behaviors within yourself that you don't want to pass down to your grandkids.

So you have an obligation to your past. You have the obligation to at the very least not bring shame to your father and his father and his father before that. You have an obligation to maintain and build upon the reputation and cachet of your name brand.

But more than that, bigger than that, you have the obligation, the duty, a responsibility to your future generations to lead a clean, successful, healthy, happy life, right now, this day. You want to build into your RNA the key traits that you want to pass down to future generations of you so that they can become a stronger, bigger, better, faster, smarter version of you and your family.

You want to do this today. You want to start now. You want to step back and refocus. Stop thinking about you, yourself, your position in life, where you are right now and what is happening to you and around you, and start looking at the bigger picture. You need to start to realize that the future is truly in your hands. You hold it. Don't mess it up.

You need to start right now becoming the person that you want your kids to be. Stop worrying about whatever it is that you're worried about and get to work. Refocus your mind on the bigger future. Focus your mind on becoming great. Take one step forward today. Do something. Work out or go for a walk. Get strong and get big. Step back from distraction and learn something new. Understand that you do have the weight of the world on your shoulders.

And take that weight.

Your life does have meaning.

Meaning is what you give life.

Your life does have a purpose.

Your purpose is tied to the connections you make with the bigger parts of your life.

Make these connections and give your life meaning.

Make these connections and find your purpose.

Superpower #15

Immortality

Life is a series of harmonic vibrations. Life, human life, can be looked at as a series of waves approaching a beach. If you step back, you can see the rhythmically placed, geographically spaced sets of waves approaching a shoreline, parallel and similar but everyone different. These waves can be modeled or described as physical things like generations.

If you look closer, you can see smaller waves riding on the bigger waves. These waves can be seen as the individual lives that cast themselves upon the beach moving in generational waves, pushing genetic changes forward and back and then forward some more.

If you step back and look at a longer timeline, you can see rhythmic tidal flows moving and changing the shoreline. These waves can be seen as countries, cultures or tribes of peoples moving over the land.

If you look even closer, you can see memetic ideas, thousands and billions of mosquito-sized ripplings riding within, on top and over the little waves riding on longer waves. These can be thought of as ideas that individual people have. Some of these ideas are as small as you thinking up a better way to fold your laundry. And some of these ideas can be as huge as understanding that F=ma.

A person and his memories can be thought of as a wave. His memories and experiences are a harmonized, acoustic resonate box, like the body of a guitar. This resonate box is your body; the vibrations inside the box are your consciousness.

Sometimes, if you're lucky, the strumming of your mind can resonate with a few other souls that harmonize with you during your life. If you work hard and are lucky, these vibrations can spread to other people in larger waves. If you are brilliant and work hard and are lucky, these cords of tones will find a harmonic resonance with families and tribes and cultures that build tremors, pulsations, and shakings that build and jump from flutters to waves, from bigger waves to tidal forces that move generations, cultures and countries.

Jesus Christ can be thought of as a wave. Elvis can be thought of as a wave. Newton was a wave.

You are a wave.

Your disturbance, your moving through life, your place on this wave will have an effect on the position, direction, and placement of the larger wave that you are part of.

Your purposeful effort in moving through life starts a wave that changes everything that is part of the larger wave that you are part of. The amount of effort you put into your life, the amount of your talent that you can leverage in application to this work, and the amount of coincidence (luck) you can grab hold of as you work will build your wave bigger and bigger.

These waves, the things you're riding, the things you're building, will have a grander effect that will propagate further and faster than your life alone.

Your family wave will move on through time as you cast your life on the beach.

Your memetic wave will ripple through time and space, adding to peaks and subtracting from valleys of other waves.

If you apply your talents, work hard and capture your luck, you will be able to make a wave that is substantial enough to carry on through time—the bigger the wave, the longer the time.

Jesus is immortal.

Elvis is immortal.

Newton is immortal.

Their memetic vibrations have harmonized with billions of souls over millions of waves.

It is up to you to decide how big a wave you want to start.

Get to work.

Your life does have meaning.

Meaning is what you give life.

Your life does have a purpose.

Your purpose is tied to the connections you make with the bigger parts of your life.

Make these connections and give your life meaning.

Make these connections and find your purpose.

So what is the takeaway of all of this? What do you do with all of this information? If you take one thing away from all of my ramblings, make it be this.

If you are having a really good day, in the middle of a really good week, of a really good month, during a really good year, go home and make love to your wife.

And hope that it sticks.

That will make a really good baby.

Do you want to keep your kids safe?

I mean, not just now when they are small, but later in life, as they grow older and get bigger.

Would you like to be able to give them some kind of way to protect themselves?

As your kids grow up and begin to spend more on their own, wouldn't you like to somehow give them a supernatural force field?

A force field that protects them and keeps them safe.

LESSON SIXTEEN

Love is letting your kids run downhill

Kids take risks.

It's like they don't get it. They don't understand the consequences. They haven't lived long enough to see what's coming. Or maybe they're not quite smart enough yet to think things through.

An older kid, an adult, stops for a moment to think things through. Like playing chess, you don't just make a move because you feel like it. You think about moves three or four moves in advance and try to predict what will happen next. You think about how your move will change your opponent's next move and how that move will impact the environment on the board.

When you're a kid, you haven't learned this strategy yet. The application of this meme hasn't made its way into your daily thought subroutine. You don't get it.

Also, you haven't been hurt. You don't know what pain is yet. If you haven't done a bunch of stuff, then you probably haven't screwed up enough. And, as the old story goes, you don't learn the lesson when things go right. You learn something when things go wrong.

So, if you haven't screwed up, you haven't learned anything.

There's an old Polish saying: "Pain is the most efficient teacher."

Oh sure, you can learn by doing. And you can learn by teaching. But if you really want to learn something, get into a high stress, extremely painful situation and mess up. That lesson you won't forget.

You always remember the questions on the exam that cost you the grade. You always remember the girl that broke your heart. You always remember the time when you pulled a wheelie and the front wheel came off.

Well, you always remember it if you live through it.

So here's the thing. You want your kids to:

A) Learn new things
B) Survive the lesson

You want your kids to be safe and stay alive, but you can't be there all the time.

I see a lot of parents hovering over their kids to keep them safe. They don't want their kids to get hurt. They walk two steps behind their kid or two steps in front and try to be a safety bubble around their kids. They try to catch them when they fall, catch anything that falls on them or stop any uncomfortable feeling from happening before it has a chance to happen.

This is a bad idea.

If you do that, if you try to keep your kids safe, your kids will never learn how to keep themselves safe.

This is what I call the Personal Safety Bubble.

One day, years ago, my wife and I were hiking with a big group of families up in the High Sierras. We were at a lake above the tree line. I don't remember how old our kids were. I don't remember exactly where we were. I do know that it must have been a long time ago because I know I could still run. Anyway, we had hiked two or three miles up to this lake. The hike was mostly above tree line, so there was no dirt. The terrain was all big, sharp, jagged, granite boulders and rubble. It was a beautiful day hike.

We played at the lake for a while, and then in the late morning, it was time to head back down to the cars. The trail was rugged and steep. We walked for a few minutes, but after a while, my kids got bored and started to jog.

At first, it was a slow, easy trot, kind of cruising down this gentle slope. But the way down was anything but gentle. The path wasn't dirt or sand. It was at best course gravel surrounded by big, sharp rocks.

I took off following them, about 10 paces behind, kind of just loping, bounding down after them. It was a beautiful, sunny, clear day in the cool, crisp air of the High Sierras.

At first, my kids were just kind of jogging. But then their sibling competition kicked in and they started to run. After ten more steps, it was a full-on race. They were now racing down this cliff.

I did my best to keep up with them, but the race was on. They were just little kids and they hadn't thought it through. One missed step, one turned ankle and they would fly halfway down the cliff, headlong at full speed into a giant boulder of sharp, solid granite.

They were bounding down the slope where each step covered maybe five or six feet. It was terrifying watching my kids run full speed, barely in control down a cliff, in the middle of the mountains, two hours from the nearest hospital.

I thought about calling them back. I thought about telling them to stop. But I just couldn't. It was too beautiful; it was just too magical, running ten steps behind my kids fearlessly running at full speed down this mountain.

The thing is—my kids felt in control. They felt perfectly safe. They weren't afraid of running down a cliff.

They didn't feel like they needed to slow down or take it easy. They were in complete command and control of their own bodies. They knew their capabilities and abilities, and they trusted themselves and their bodies.

You need to be able to encourage that feeling. You need to instill in them their own understanding of who they are and what they can do. You need to encourage them to discover their own sense of safety and security. If they think they can do it, let them try. They will learn for themselves what they can do and what they can't do. They will learn for themselves when they are safe or when they are at risk according to their own confidence in their own physical ability.

It is very important for you to let your kids develop these skills on their own.

It is important because you know that you are not going to be next to them all the time or for very long. They will need this crucial skill, and they need to learn that it is their responsibility to learn this skill now when they are young.

They need to learn that they are responsible for themselves, their safety and their own personal security. It is their number one job, their number one priority to keep themselves alive.

And if you disrupt this personal learning process, if you keep them from getting hurt, if you inhibit the development of their own personal safety bubble, you will be robbing them of this critical life lesson.

You have to let them try and fail. You have to give them a long leash. That leash has to be just long enough for them to maybe get hurt but not too long that they end up killing themselves.

You need to do this so that they learn how to keep themselves safe.

This is really hard to do. This is really hard to watch. It is the hardest thing in the world to see your child hurt or in pain. But you have to do it to keep them safe.

At the end of the run, we met the other families at the parking lot. It took a while for them to hike down. When the other mothers finally made it back to the cars, they were crazy. They were screaming at me, "What the hell were you doing? That was dangerous. Why didn't you stop them? That was insane. You are a horrible father. You should have done something. Running down a cliff like that; they could have killed themselves!"

My wife was pretty pissed too. She told me that that was sketchy. She said that that was really scary. She asked me why I let them do that. I told her that I just couldn't stop them. That it was just too much fun. I had to reassure her that we were fine and everything was okay. She was pretty shaken up.

And she told me, "Well, I guess love is letting your kids run downhill."

This has become one of our family mottoes.

"Love is letting your kids run downhill."

It means that you have to let your kids take risks. You have to let them explore the boundaries of their own personal safety. You have to encourage them to take personal responsibility for their bodies and their safety. You have to give them a long leash—a leash that is long enough to let them perhaps hurt themselves but not long enough to kill themselves.

This is hard to do. It is scary. But it must be done. It must be done if you want them, in the long run, to be safe. It must be done so that they learn firsthand their own personal safety bubble. And they can only do this if you can allow them to be at risk.

You can keep your kids safe.

You can help them learn to stay safe as they grow older and get bigger.

You can give them a way to protect themselves.

As your kids grow up and move out into the world, give them a supernatural force field.

Teach them to discover for themselves their very own personal safety bubble.

Let your kids run, full speed, downhill.

Superpower #16

Force Field

Allowing your kids to develop their own personal safety bubble is like giving them a force field. It is your job to enable their force field, encourage their force field and help them build a force field.

Teach them that they are personally responsible for their own safety now and always.

Teach them to save themselves.

When our kids were small, we were lucky enough to go on a couple of wild adventures. One summer my wife and I decided to each take a month off and go on a long road trip. We packed up the car with our tent, our backpacks, and our mountain bikes and meandered our way north. We camped here and there. We stayed with some friends in Montana, and we mountain biked in Jackson Hole. That turned out to be just a little bit too much for us.

Jackson Hole is a big, scary mountain. Mountain biking was kind of a new thing, and they had just opened up the mountain to bikes in the summer. We could load our bikes on a chairlift and take them up the mountain. But they really hadn't made any real bike trails to ride down. You were just kind of on your own going through the forest down this really hairy ski run.

Keep in mind, our son was seven and our daughter was ten. And the crappy little bikes that we picked up from Walmart weren't really made for this level of downhill. Both my son and my daughter had some spectacular falls, but it was I that got the worst of it.

Halfway down one run, I took a shortcut through a clearing of high grass, hit a ditch, fell and ended up breaking a couple of ribs. That pretty much put me out of commission for the rest of the trip. I rode down to the bar, drank half a dozen shots of Jack and went to lie on a glacier-fed, half-frozen Wyoming lake.

A couple days later we were camping in Yellowstone. We knew some folks that worked there and they gave us a map of all of the cool secret places that most people don't know about. One of those places was the Madison River Turnout on Highway 191. There is a place near there where hot springs bubble up at the edge of the Madison River.

There is a little turnout where you can park your car and walk down to the river. The Madison River, by the way, is a mad, mountain-cold, rushing river. Off to one side is a little place dug out by the locals. It is kind of like a Jacuzzi where there is a small pile of round river rocks formed into a kind of a wall that separates the cold river water on one side and the hot, steaming spring water on the other. There were maybe a dozen other people there. They had all found this cool secret hangout. It is a wonderful place to lounge in a lovely all-natural outdoor bath. The spring water was kind of too hot, but the cold river water trickled through the rock wall to bring it to a manageable temperature.

Well, our son Gus was in a good mood. He was climbing on the pile of rocks between the cold, rushing river and the hot, bubbling water when he went just a little too far. He slipped and fell into the river. He was quickly rushed downstream into the rapids.

It was horrifying. It looked really bad.

I instantly tried to jump up out of my bath but was quickly reminded that I had two broken ribs.

There was nothing I could do.

My son was being swept away into the rapids.

My son screamed, "Daddy, HELP!"

And I looked at him horrified.

I screamed back, "I can't! I'm hurt. You have to save yourself."

Everyone in the Jacuzzi was horrified.

But then a magical thing happened. My son put his head down and started swimming through the rushing current towards the bank of the river. He grabbed a rock and pulled himself towards the edge. He grabbed another rock and pulled himself out.

It was incredible. We were all stunned. He saved himself.

He stood knee deep at the edge of the freezing river and pumped his hands over his head. It was awesome.

It was like he was some kind of super-kid out of a movie. The crowd went wild.

We looked at each other in shock. One of the other dads said to me, "That was incredible?"

And I thought, "Wow, I've got badass kids."

You have to teach your kids about personal responsibility. You have to teach your kids that they are responsible for their own personal safety—full stop, no exceptions.

You have to let them know that they are ultimately responsible for their own wellbeing. Teach them to never count on anyone else for their personal security. Never depend on the police to save you. Never count on your neighbors or your community or your village to save you. You need to teach them that they have to be competent and capable enough to save themselves in every situation.

Don't even let them think that they can count on you.

Teach them to work out every day and stay strong. They have to be able to take care of themselves. If trouble comes their way, which it probably will, they have to be able to handle it.

Teach them not to let go of their personal safety or security. Never put your life in someone else's hands. Never count on anyone to protect you. Or save you. Or rescue you. Let them know that they are in charge and they need to have Plan A, Plan B, and Plan C in place before they ever even start to put themselves at risk.

This helps with two things: first, for you, it keeps them safe. You know you don't have to be there all the time. You know that they can handle themselves in any situation. You don't have to worry and hover.

Second, for them, it gives them a huge amount of confidence. When they get big and strong, they will know that they will be able to handle problems as they come. When they save themselves from the rapids, they will stand tall. They will walk differently. They will move through life with confidence. The sooner you can encourage this kind of thinking, the more of a multiplying effect it will have and the greater the impact there will be over their lifetime.

Teach your kids to be self-reliant.

Encourage your kids to take big risks.

Raise badass kids.

You can keep your kids safe.

You can help them learn to stay safe as they grow older and get bigger.

You can give them a way to protect themselves.

As your kids grow up and move out into the world, give them a supernatural force field.

Teach them to discover for themselves their very own personal safety bubble.

Let your kids run, full speed, downhill.

Some kids just seem to be 45 when they are 14?

Isn't it amazing when you see children that have poise and confidence under pressure?

Like the kids that compete in the National Spelling Bee. They are up there on stage. They are in front of the world. They are under immense pressure.

And they have to think.

The kids that win are the ones that can perform their best under intense pressure.

Wouldn't you like to give your kids that?

Would you like to give your kids poise and confidence?

Would you like to find a way to give your kids the ability to perform at their highest level under intense pressure?

LESSON SEVENTEEN

No problem, Dad, I got this

As soon as we could, we got our kids involved in team sports. There are all kinds of reasons to encourage your kids to do sports. Some of the typical things are well known. It's a great way to keep your kids active. It's a great way to help them find new friends. It's a great way for them to learn at an early age how to work as a team.

And it's a great way to teach passion. When your kids start to play a sport from the time they are very young, they learn the sport from the fundamentals. They learn the intricate details of each position. They learn how much work it takes to be really good at something. And the longer they work at the sport, the more time they have invested in the sport, the more they will come to love the sport. This love of sport will translate into a lifetime of interest and passion. This common understanding and ability they can share with all kinds of people from old friends to strangers you meet on the street.

During the World Cup, for instance, you can stop pretty much any person on any street in any country of the world and ask, "Hey, where can we watch the game tonight?" Ninety percent of the time the people will think for a moment then start pointing down the street to the local pub. Or if they are really friendly, they will invite you over to their local pre-game party. This is a great way to make connections and establish empathy through the common understanding of a sport.

It is also a great way to instill in them an active, healthy lifestyle. This early adoption of sports will keep them moving and healthy their whole lives.

But there's more to it than that.

One time, when my daughter was 10 years old, we were playing an AYSO regional championship game in Pasadena, California. Our team had had a stellar year. We had a great group of girls, a fantastic bunch of parents and a crazy coach. He had broken his leg halfway through the season and attended each game and practice in a wheelchair.

The game was a nail-biter. I think we ended double overtime with a 2-2 tie. It was time for penalty kicks. I hate this part of the game. It is a real shame when the win or loss of an entire season comes down to a shootout.

My daughter was in the goal. She was big for her age, strong and fearless. Goalie was the perfect position for her. But defending against PKs is no fun. It is almost impossible to stop a well-struck ball into the lower corner of the net.

If the game is tied at the end of regular play, both teams move off to their sidelines kind of like a timeout. The girls huddle around the coach and the parents usually bring their daughters water. The coach puts the girls in a line and assigns them their shot order.

I was scared as hell. I knew there was a lot of pressure on my daughter. It's bad enough being a kicker in this situation. You knew you had to score a point to win the game. Your whole team was counting on you. You only get one shot and you don't want to mess it up. Being the goalie, on the other hand, is crazy hard. You don't usually get the chance to kick; you only get the chance to defend. You get ten chances to screw up. You have to save the game over and over and over again.

I knew what was at stake here. If we won the game, our team moved on to sectionals. If we lost, our season was over. My daughter had to stop at least a couple of point-blank strikes from ten yards away.

I was a mess. I was shaking as I handed my daughter a bottle of water. I quickly tried to give my daughter some last minute advice. I was mumbling something like, "Don't think. Just react. Pick a side and go for the ball."

My daughter smiled over her brow and held up her hand to kind of shush me.

She looked me in the eye and said, almost in a whisper,

"Shh – Shh – Shh.

Calm down, Dad.

Don't worry.

It's going to be okay.

I got this."

She trotted off pulling on her goalie gloves.

I was stunned. I couldn't believe what I just saw. She had such composure. She was so relaxed and sure of herself. She didn't feel any pressure. She was just having fun. As I stood there with my mouth open, she skipped away towards the goal.

She put her heels on the line as the other team lined up.

The kicking started and it was crazy. We scored; then the other team scored. Then we scored and the other team scored. Then we scored; then the other team scored. This went on and on. Each time a point is scored the pressure goes up. Each time you have fewer and fewer chances to win the game. By the tenth player on each team, the game was still tied.

In this situation, after all of the other players take their turns, if the game is still tied, the goalies have to go. So the goalie from the other team took off her jersey and gloves and lined up in front of the ball.

The whistle blew, the ball was kicked, my daughter dove—and caught the ball, denying the other team a goal.

But it wasn't over. After 21 players the game was still tied. My daughter had to kick the ball into the back of the net to win the game—and the season. The pressure was intense.

The crowd was silent. The other team's goalie put back on her jersey and got back in the goal.

The whistle blew. My daughter approached the ball and smack. The ball flew past the goalie and into the back of the net. It was crazy. The crowd went wild.

I know a lot of guys that spend a lot of money going to every Laker game. But I can tell you, of all that time and all that energy watching someone you don't know play a game, there is nothing like the feeling you get watching your kid score a goal to win the game, the series and the season.

The thing is, with all the workouts and all the practices and all the games, the thing you get is this. You get to give your kids the opportunity to face intense pressure—to perform under intense pressure at a young age.

What you want is a series of small steps. What you are looking for is a system of incremental successful steps. It is the simple, small step of a successful practice—the simple, small step of scoring a goal or deflecting a penalty kick. The simple, small step of winning a game. That gives your children the confidence to approach high-stress situations with poise. That gives your children the ability to walk up to you moments before the biggest play of their lives and say,

"No problem, Dad. I got this."

You can train your children to perform at their highest level under intense pressure.

The kids that win are the ones that can perform their best under stress.

You can give your kids poise and confidence and grace under pressure.

Would you like to find a way to give your kids the ability to perform at their highest level?

Put your kids in team sports and encourage them to compete.

Guide your kids up onto the biggest stage in front of the biggest crowds early in life so they get used to being in front of people.

Shepherd your children into competitive environments at an early age.

Set them up in training situations where they can make a series of incremental successful steps.

And give them training that encourages competition.

Superpower #17

Poise

I like to do crazy things. I like jumping off really high bridges. I like skiing off cliffs and jumping out of airplanes. The first time you jump off a cliff, it is very exciting. It is very new. Your mind has to cope with a huge amount of sensory data. But there's a problem.

After I left Vail with my leg in a cast, I didn't ski again for more than ten years. The crazy thing is the next day I skied, more than a decade later, was one of the best ski days of my life. It was like I had been practicing, in my mind, the whole time.

This is how it always goes. You try something once, you think about it, you run through your experience over and over again in your mind, and then when you're done you try it again. The second time is easier, but when trying some crazy stunt, doing it the first time always sucks.

There are a couple parts to this problem.

The first part is the newness. This is the thing where you're doing something new for the first time. When you do something for the first time, you kind of stumble through it. You don't really know what you're doing, so you just throw your body down the hill or off the cliff and hope that your physical reaction time is quick enough to keep you from dying.

Then, your mind reruns the tape; it rewinds your mental memory tape and then replays the incident over and over again to refine your approach. You are basically just running simulated practice reruns of the incident. Your mind can do this consciously if you focus or it will do this in your sleep if the first experience was traumatic enough. The second time you try this stunt, it will be a lot easier to do. Even if you don't do it again for years, the next time you do it, whatever it was, it will be easier to do.

So the question is: How can you get it better the first time?

Another important part of this problem is being able to think. It is hard to think under pressure. The more pressure, the harder it is to think. Sometimes, when you're under enough pressure, you just freeze like a narcoleptic goat. Your mind can't think at all. This happened to me the first time I jumped out of a plane.

The first time you jump out of a plane, the physical sensation is really overwhelming. First, you've got the training. You spend a day in a classroom going over and over what is about to happen to you. You have an instructor that is there to basically tell you over and over again, "Okay, if you do this you are going to die and if you do that you are going to die and if you don't do this you are going to die and if you don't do that you are going to die. After a couple hours of that, you should be pretty well convinced that you are going to die whatever you do.

Then you've got the garb. They dress you up in a funny protective bunch of safety gear. You've got the flight suit and the gloves. You've got the goggles and the helmet. You've got the special boots and the magic underwear. And then, on top of everything else, you've got this twenty-pound parachute that goes over everything, latches it down and cinches it up until you can hardly breathe. With all of this gear and garb, there is at least one layer of plastic or nylon or fiberglass between you and the outside world. You feel completely insulated and removed from anything real.

Then you get shoved inside a small plane that usually has the doors or the windows removed so you feel like you're right out there in space and completely exposed.

Then you take off and start blasting down the runway at a hundred miles an hour.

Then you go butt-ass up in the air something like a bazillion feet with the doors off, the windows open, the wind screaming by and nothing—and I do mean nothing at all—underneath you.

The sensations, the physical inputs are intense. Every part of your body is being assaulted. You are jostled around. You are blown around. You are pushed around. You are screamed at. Your eyes are screaming. Your ears are screaming, your stomach is screaming, and you've got some part of last night's dinner stuck up in one of the corners of your left sinus.

It is hard to think when all of your senses are being overwhelmed at once.

But you have to think. You have to remember to do this and don't do that.

You have to remember to pull the ripcord and save yourself.

And then they tell you to jump.

And it's fun.

The first time I jumped I froze.

I remember stepping out of the plane. We were in a Cessna 172. That is one of the medium-sized small planes. It is a wing-over plane, so the wing is over the body of the aircraft. There is a crossbar that goes diagonally between the bottom of the wing and the bottom of the fuselage. On that crossbar, there is a little peddle about the size of the peddle from a bicycle. I remember stepping out of the plane, into the 130 mph airstream, grabbing on the crossbar and standing with all my weight on that little pedal.

Your sensory perception at this point is very small if you haven't done this before. It's like trying to see the world while looking through a drinking straw. I think what happens here is that you are experiencing too much. The sound is so loud because you are standing unsecured in hurricane strength winds. Your visual cortex is bombarded by images of the sky, the horizon and the ground 3000 feet below. And the skin of your entire body is sending signals to your brain that it is being violently thrashed by the wind whipping your jumpsuit while standing on this little, flimsy pedal.

All of these data inputs are smashing together into the base of your brain all at the same time. You are literally having information overload. Your consciousness just can't keep up. So it basically just shuts down.

I remember the first time I was standing on that little pedal and the instructor yelled, "One, two, three, jump!"

The funny part is I don't really remember what happened next. You would think that in that kind of dramatic, high stress, first in a lifetime, crazy experience you would remember something, but I just don't. My memories did not record. I think I was having such sensory overload that my mind was unable to make sense of anything. I really don't remember anything until the parachute popped above my head and my body came to what seemed like a full stop, like being jerked out of the sky.

Then everything was relatively quiet. Everything was still. You could look around and hear again. I kind of woke up and realized that I had been out of touch for several seconds there. That is a really bad several seconds to give up. Those were the critical several seconds that I needed to be aware. That was the exact time that I needed to be present. That was the time that I could have done something to save my life. But I wasn't there. I was overwhelmed. I was frozen. Like a lump of clay. Like a deer in the headlights.

Of course the next time I jumped it wasn't such a big deal. My mind had been through this once before. It knew what to expect. It knew what to focus on. It knew what data points were important and what inputs it could ignore. The next time I jumped I remembered the whole thing. I was there. I was present. I could consciously do everything I needed to do. I felt like I could easily pull my own ripcord or deploy my reserve chute without any problem.

My mind had fixed itself because I had been through this before.

And that's the point. Training is key. You want to give your kids the biggest, fastest, most intense sensation training you can afford.

If they express an interest in any kind of activity or sport, do whatever you can to encourage that sport.

Whether it be rock climbing or windsurfing, parasailing or skydiving, you want to get them into high altitude, high adventure, high-speed experiences as soon as you can and as young as they can be.

This gets them used to and experienced with high-intensity environments.

And this helps them be able to cope with new first-time experiences more competently.

You can train your children to perform at their highest level under intense pressure.

The kids that win are the ones that can perform their best under stress.

You can give your kids poise and confidence and grace.

Put your kids in team sports and encourage them to compete.

Shepherd your children into competitive environments at an early age.

Set them up in training situations where they can make a series of incremental successful steps.

And give them training that encourages competition.

Ever wonder what it would be like to be

bulletproof?

Ever imagine what it would be like to casually

walk into a gunfight with complete confidence,

knowing that you are untouchable?

Knowing that no one can hurt you?

Wouldn't you love to give your kids that kind of

power, that kind of courage?

Would you like to be able to give your children the

ability to be bulletproof?

Would you like to teach your kids resiliency and

strength in the face of disaster and

disappointment?

LESSON EIGHTEEN

Talk about losing

A while back I had a job. The money was good. The job was fun. I was relatively good at it. It was mildly fulfilling. The problem was, the job was in San Diego, two hours from home. I felt guilty for being away. I felt bad about not being around for my kids. I felt so guilty, in fact, that I would just buy random crap thinking that it might fill the hole left by my absence. I call these purchases guilt buys. It's the idea of being a good dad $500 at a time.

One of these guilt buys was to pay for a year of club volleyball for my daughter. In Southern California, there are lots and lots of things to do. Swimming, soccer, golf, tennis, the list goes on and on. If you're a girl and tall, one of the big ticket items on this list is volleyball.

It was stupid expensive, but I figured, hey, we've got the money, and she needs something to do while I'm at work in San Diego, so what the hell? Let's pony up the cash and pay for her to join a club team.

Well, my daughter loved it. She loved the whole thing—the kids, the comradery, the competition, the idea that she got to do something new and different, above and beyond the stuff that her friends at school got to do.

Each year it got bigger, more elaborate and more expensive. It turned into a quasi-full time gig. She had practices three times a week and tournaments every weekend. When she got into high school, she joined the high school team. This enlarged the commitment. Between her high school team and her club team, she was now playing volleyball full time. If we added in the travel time, driving back and forth to practice and the weekend tournaments, she was spending about twenty hours a week playing volleyball.

The high school season started in the summer before the start of school and ended in the late fall, depending on how well your team was doing. If your HS team kept winning, you kept playing through November and December. The club team starts up in November and ends in late June or early July with the Junior Olympics. When we looked at our long-term annual calendar, my daughter had about two weeks off each year. Not counting Christmas, we would get maybe one week off in November and one week off in July.

The older she got, the more intense the competition became—not just competition between different teams at the tournaments but competition within her club team for her position and her playing time during the games. The inter-team rivalry was the worst. The competition was cut-throat. Some of the parents of the other girls were grotesque, horrible people, but let's not talk about that.

Maybe two or three times a year we would have to fly off to some Junior National Qualifier in some town like Reno or Cleveland. These tournaments were incredible. Tens of thousands of teenage girls packed into a convention hall the size of a small city or a regional airport. The tournament would usually last three days. The first two days are pool play where your team has to play everyone in your pool. If you win all of your matches on the first day, your team moves up. If you lose, you move down. If you win all of your matches on the second day, you move into the Gold Bracket. The Teams in the Gold Bracket play for a chance to fly to Orlando and play at the Junior Olympics. Basically, you want to win every game and every match.

Being from Southern Cal, the hot-bed of girls volleyball, and being from the South Bay, the center of Southern Cal, our teams were usually pretty good. That kind of pressure and competition forged the girls and the teams into hardened volleyball machines.

One year we were up in Reno, I think, maybe it was San Diego. We had a contentious team. The club was okay, the coaches were good enough and the girls were really good. There was a lot of tension between the girls. It is hard to keep a bunch of teenage girls confined, competing and focused on something other than killing each other. We had made it into the Gold Bracket, and we were playing on the last day for all the marbles. We had won our first couple matches and had made it to the semifinals. These matches were best of three. So you need to win two games. If you win one and lose one, you have to play a third game.

By the time you get to this position in the season, you have invested almost 1000 hours over the year into volleyball. By the time you get to play this game, you have worked your ass off. You have fought through the pain, the fatigue, the pressure and the team politics. By the time you get to this game, you have beaten all of the lesser teams. The girls on the other side of the net are your peers, tall, fit, strong and vicious. They all hate to lose and they all want to win.

This game was intense. Our team won the first game, but we lost the second. The match was going to three. The teams were fairly matched. It was a good team and it wasn't going to be a blowout. The game was point for point. We would make a point and then the other team would make a point—9-8, 9-9, 9-10, 10-10...

In the third game of a match, the game is to 15 and you have to win by two points. This game was tight. We got to 15 and then the opposing team got to 16, and since you have to win by two, they just kept going. We got to 16 and they would get to 17.

They – Just – Kept – Going.

They would serve and we would score, and then we would serve and they would score. Our girls were exhausted, but the adrenaline kept them at their peak. In the bleachers, it was a different story. The parents were a mess. No one was sitting down. Everyone was screaming. Blood and sweat and drool were flying every which way. The dads were pacing the floor.

Some couldn't watch. It was too intense; they turned their backs or covered their faces. The hopes and dreams of the tourney, the year, the season and their daughter's chance at a D1 college scholarship hung in the balance of this next serve, this next spike or this next dig. One dad even had to lie down behind the bleachers. He thought he might be having a heart attack. We ignored him.

In the end – we lost.

It was a crushing defeat. Not because we weren't good enough. Not because someone screwed up. Not because we hadn't worked hard enough or that we weren't prepared. We just lost; the flick of a wrist, the roll of the ball, the call of a referee, something happened and we lost. I think the final score was 27-29, a full 26 points beyond a typical third game.

There were tears and anger, but our girls gracefully met at the net to shake hands, "Good game – good game – good game." The girls them went off for the debrief with their coach.

Walking away from that game, I was a mess. I think I was crying harder than my daughter. I turned to one of the other dads and said, "Can you believe that? That was incredible. Have you ever seen anything like it?" He said, "No, I haven't."

I said, "This is what it's all about, this, right here. This is why we are investing all of our time and all of our money, to get to this point, to work this hard, to play that well, under that much pressure, and lose."

I asked my friend, "Have you ever been in a position like that? Where it's all on the line and you have to keep your head and compete on a national level? I have never been in that position. And our kids already have. They are so young and they have already been put into an incredibly difficult situation, under so much pressure, and lost. This is what it's all about. They have learned that they can take a loss. They can face defeat. It's not going to crush them. It's not going to kill them. It's not going to stop them. It is this kind of situation that makes them stronger, makes them tougher, makes them more resilient, makes them better people, makes them fully human. They have already climbed that mountain.

They have already faced that demon. If you wait until you're our age and something like that happens to you for the first time, it will set you back. For them, it's just going to be a tough next couple of days and then it will be on to the next thing, the next workout, the next season."

I told my friend, "I am happy for them. This has been a good day."

You'll never be bulletproof.

But your kids will be.

You can teach your kids how to be resilient and strong in the face of disaster and disappointment.

You can give your kids that kind of power, that kind of courage.

Give your children the ability to be bulletproof.

Push your kids into situations where they can win—and where they can lose.

Don't comfort the loss.

Teach your children to use the pain of loss as motivation to work harder and move higher.

Let your kids lose early and often and push them forward.

Teach your children that every loss is just another step towards success.

And that pain is just the feeling of weakness leaving their body.

Bulletproof

You need to get involved.

The first time we got our kids into sports, it was through AYSO, the American Youth Soccer Association. The first year I didn't really do anything. They ask you to help out. They asked for assistant coaches and referees. They needed a team mom and other volunteers. I was really busy and working full time.

There was this one guy. His name was John. He tried to get me to volunteer. He was a tall, super skinny, older dad. We had a lot in common and hung out together. But I looked at this guy helping out with his little girl's soccer team and thought, Hmm, that guy must be kind of a loser if he has enough time to coach his kid's team. I'm important. I'm working my ass off. I don't have time for that.

So I didn't volunteer. I didn't help out. I was an absentee parent. I let all the other guys do all the work. I saw some guys refereeing two and three other games on Saturday. As a volunteer referee, you were obligated to referee one game per weekend. Why would anyone do more than that? I thought that was crazy.

As the season went on and I sat next to John on the sidelines, I began to see that John was even busier than I was. He was running a company and buying a house and trying to figure out when to put his younger daughter in soccer. He decided that the only way he could do it was to become a coach. If he was the coach for both teams, then he could set the practices to fit his schedule.

John also decided that I had to be his assistant coach. He kept bugging me until I reluctantly succumbed to the peer pressure of pulling my load. He kept saying, "Dude, you've got to help out and it's going to be a blast."

I was on the outside looking in –

But here's the thing, there's more to it than that. What I learned that first year, what I couldn't see from the outside, was the most important part of being your kid's soccer coach.

It wasn't that you get to set your practice schedule. It was that you got to spend an extra two or three hours a week with your kids.

I didn't realize from the outside how much that means.

First, you get to teach your kids the bigger process of doing something. You have to get all of the stuff, all of the gear, the cones and the jerseys, the balls and all of the other junk that you need to run the practices. You need to organize everything and get it out and put it away and have a place for it. It's a process. And this process is a great lesson to teach.

My mom used to tell me that to do anything exciting you have to do a lot of work. Let's say you want to go skiing. It usually takes a day to get out all of your ski gear from wherever it is stored in the rafters of the garage, clean it up, check it out, make sure it works, and then pack it into the car. Then it takes another day to drive or fly to the ski resort. You might get to ski for one or two days, and then you have to go through the same two-day process, driving home, unpacking your gear, cleaning it off and storing it away at the end of your trip.

Any fun thing you do takes at least three times more time to get ready to do it, do it, and then undo it than it takes just to do it. The more fun the thing is, the more work it is to do that fun thing. Let's say you want to race your yacht to Hawaii in the Trans-Pac. It will take months, maybe years to get yourself and your boat ready for that race. If you are fast, the race might take only eight or nine days. But the preparation is crazy.

Think about the craziest fun thing you can think of. Think about going to the moon. It took us about ten years to get ready to go to the moon. How long were we there? Couple days? Add it all up; the more fun and exciting something is to do, the more time and effort you have to spend preparing for and recovering from the adventure.

Getting directly involved with something like soccer with your kids is a great way to teach your kids this important lesson. Don't pay someone else to do it with your kids. Get involved and do it yourself with your kids. Use this structure to teach your kids how to get organized, how to organize an adventure. Get your kids to help with the process. Put them in charge of all of the stuff. Make a space for all of the balls and the bags, the cones and the cleats and the jerseys. And then get your kids to help you organize the stuff. Make this chore part of the fun.

This is important because it is part of a larger lesson.

It goes back to the Love Bank idea.

Every minute that you get to spend with your kids is a gift. That next hour that you get to spend with your son might be the most valuable hour of his life. Every moment you get to spend with your daughter is like money in the bank. Except, it is better than that; it is more valuable than money.

Good relationships with your children are some of the most valuable experiences that a human can have.

These relationships are built one minute at a time.

Every minute that you can spend with your kids getting ready for an adventure and cleaning up afterward is another minute that you get to put in the Love Bank. And it teaches your kids how to have adventures.

Do not shy away from competition. Don't try and shelter your kids from adversity.

Find a way to get your kids into competitive situations as soon as you can.

Look for situations where they can win and lose.

Take the time to teach your kids how to prepare for grand adventures.

A constant chain of small wins will boost their confidence.

A once in a while crushing defeat will build their character.

Experiencing a crushing defeat when they are young will make them into superheroes.

It will make them bulletproof.

Section 4

COMING HOME

A while back my wife was working in Pasadena. I had a job down in San Diego and we lived in Alta Dena. I was working 100 miles away. We were living near L.A., and I was working as a construction project manager. I would wake up every Monday at 3 am so that I could beat the traffic and get to my desk by 6. I was managing a dozen or so multi-million-dollar construction projects inside a hospital—anything from a new CT suite to a 160-car parking structure. It was a full-time double plus job. I usually worked half days, from 6 am to 6 pm, but at least twice a week I worked till 9 pm. It was easy then because I had no life and no family in San Diego. I would start work at 6 am on Monday morning and work straight through until Friday afternoon. Then I would drive home to Alta Dena to spend the weekend with my family.

Although the money was good, the job was brutal. I was paid to be an asshole. My employer expected me to command using fear and intimidation. I couldn't be friendly or friends with anybody. If there was a problem on the job site, it was my job to find the guy that screwed up and scream at him or fire him. My boss thought that this was the best way to make everybody pay attention and work hard. If I didn't threaten potential violence towards the people that worked for me, I would be fired by my boss for being too soft. And I was constantly reminded that if anything big went wrong on one of my job sites, I would be the first guy that gets the ax.

I worked for a guy that liked to fire people. He fired people all the time. He would fire at least one contractor, inspector, compliance officer or project manager each month to keep everybody on their toes. I was fired from that job three times. Uncle Bob would call me into his office, rip me a new one for some perceived mismanagement or another, tell me to pack up my things and never come back. Then, come Sunday night he would call me at home and demand that I be in his office at six in the morning to talk about a new project.

Being a PM on just one job site was stressful. I was managing 16 sites. The pressure was always on.

The upside about working all the time far from home was that I made a lot of money. I had the position and the power and the prestige. I had the car and the clothes and the respect (or fear) of my peers.

The downside was that it was hell on my family. Although we had plenty of money to pay for the extra help, my wife had to take up the slack at home. She had a full-time job and had to juggle two kids without me around. She would work double time to get the kids up, feed them, dress them and get them to daycare. She would work a full day and then have to summon her energy to leave work, pick the kids up from the afterschool program, drive them home, feed them, do homework, bathe them, and put them to bed; she would then have to spend another couple hours finishing the work that she hadn't gotten done that day at her job.

I would come home on the weekend, feeling guilty that I wasn't there all week, to an exhausted wife and grumpy kids. Because of my guilt, I would try to be over-enthusiastically happy. I would grab the kids and whisk them away to dinner and a movie and just generally use a party to try and make everybody feel better.

This didn't work. The reality was that to make her life work, my wife had to maintain a strict schedule. She had her timing down pat—up at seven, to school by eight, to work by nine, rewind everything and to bed by eight again. I would come home and screw all of that up. Then she would have to stumble through Monday and Tuesday trying to get the kids back on schedule. I, on the other hand, was just Mr. Party. I would come home and screw everything up and then I would leave. The self-imposed forced happiness would make the kids feel better and let me feel less guilty, but in the end, what it did was piss off my wife. And that was a very bad thing.

That wasn't the worst part of it, though. The worst part of this situation was the distance. I was far away all week.

I found that it was much easier to assume an accepted role of a man with a job with money and power and prestige. People understood what I did and how I fit into an easily defined position in society. If I told someone what I did, they could quickly make sense of who I was and what the rest of my life was like. That kind of compliance felt good. It was easier for me to assume this role and let my wife struggle with her place as a mom and a wife with a job. In a way, I was passing off most of the really difficult stresses of life to my wife.

But I knew it wasn't right. I could feel every time I came home from San Diego my kids were a little bit further away. I could feel this distance. I could feel the separation. I didn't like it. I thought, Really, what am I doing? Did I really have kids so I could pay someone else to raise them? Was that my plan? My wife was unhappy; my kids were unhappy. It was easy for me, but deep down I was unhappy.

At first, each time I came home there would be a big greeting. The kids would scream, "Dad's home!" and rush out to hug me. But each time, every Friday, I could feel a distance growing. Each Friday the enthusiasm was a little less. It went from "Dad's home!" to "Hi Dad." It went from big hugs to a standoffish wave. It was weird how I could feel this distance.

And each Friday the drive home was horrible. The traffic was bad. The trip took about five hours. The whole time I would stew in my car. I would sit there and dread what was about to happen. I would fear the future memory of the moment that I arrived. I would fear the moment when I got home and saw my kids. How would they react? What would they do this time? I knew it wasn't right. I wasn't being a good husband or a good father.

On Sunday night I would start dreading it again. I would dread the drive down to San Diego. I would dread the week at work and I would dread the next week's drive home. During the week I would stumble through my work days with an unenthusiastic mumble.

This all came to a head during one of our weekly project manager meetings. These meetings were a sweaty affair. There were about a dozen PMs working for Uncle Bob. Most of these guys were big, burly men in their fifties that had come up through the construction trade. They all had big, heavy hands with hardened, scarred fingers. They were all tough guys, but in front of Uncle Bob, they sweat.

During the meeting, each PM would give a rundown of each of his projects. Each guy would come to the meeting with stacks of three-ring binders ready to supply Uncle Bob with any factual detail that he might demand. Each guy would have a single piece of paper with bullet points for Uncle Bob. Each guy wore a white shirt and a tie. We would each sit in the same place at the same table in the same conference room. We would start on the left and go clockwise around the table. There was no small talk before the meeting. No one made eye contact. Everyone kept their heads down. No one dared to look at Uncle Bob. And the sweat poured down their backs.

It was really very simple. When it came to be your turn, you just stated the project name and the billing account number made a brief statement about where the project was on its timeline and said that the project was on schedule and within the budget.

Uncle Bob would interrupt. One of the PMs would start running down his projects and Uncle Bob would just scream, "STOP! Where is 2743?" referring to the billing account number. The PM would freeze and reach for one of his three-ring binders. He would then start describing the project and telling us exactly what was happening on the project that day. Uncle Bob would listen for a couple seconds and then say something like, "Shut up. Next." The PM would close his binder and the next PM would start his rundown.

This week when it came to me I was ready. I had all of my three-ring binders and my one page of bullet points. Before I even began, Uncle Bob said, "Where is 7556?" I reached for my binder on a new surgical recovery room being built in one of the hospitals. I said that everything was on schedule except that there was a minor problem in the bathroom.

It seems that the tile pattern in the bathroom was messed up. The construction documents called for a black, red, white pattern and the contractor laid the tiles red, black, white.

I told Uncle Bob that the guy laying the tile was confused; instead of laying the tiles from left to right, he laid the tile from right to left. A couple of the other PMs let out a half-swallowed chuckle.

Uncle Bob went off. He let me know in no uncertain terms that this miss-implementation proved that I wasn't paying attention, that this was my fault—that I was incompetent and that the entire project would probably have to be torn out and redone.

I kind of laughed and said, "But – it's just tile."

Everybody in the room froze.

A moment too late I realized that this was the wrong thing to say.

And, I felt the sweat run down my back.

Uncle Bob pounded the table and screamed, "Do you think this is funny? Do you think this is funny? You're fired. Collect your trash, empty your desk, and get out of my conference room."

This was not funny.

In shock, I stood up and left the room. I cleaned out my desk, packed my car and got on the freeway.

About halfway home I woke up.

This slap hurt.

The cars on the freeway were stopped. They were parked. They weren't moving. I was stuck in a parking lot—on the freeway—halfway between hell and hell.

I was stunned. I was exhausted. I thought about my life and looked at myself in the rearview mirror.

I looked around at all these other dads, sitting right next to me but a world away, in the same place, at the same time, in the same traffic, going nowhere. They were all burnt. They were all fried. They were all empty.

We all looked the same. Maybe we all felt the same. We were each a Clark Kent, a mild-mannered, worthless dweeb with no purpose, compulsion, meaning or reason.

I just sat in my car in shock.

I had tried to make it work.
I had made a lot of money.

I had been that guy with the position and the power and the prestige and the fear of my peers.

But it didn't work.

My wife hated me. My kids hated me.

And worst of all –

I hated me.

The ability to concentrate for long periods of time is very difficult. Intense concentration is physically exhausting. Your brain consumes about 20% of your body's energy. Thinking for eight hours is equivalent to running ten kilometers. The brain is just another muscle. The harder you work it, the bigger it gets.

You need to be in good shape to be able to maintain deep thought for any period of time. But this kind of shape is different from the physical shape of running or lifting or working out. This is a kind of mental conditioning. To have the ability to think about one thing, very deeply, for long periods of time, you need to be in really good mental shape.

How do you get your kids to work that hard? How do you get your kids to sit in a chair for hours on end and concentrate on one thing? How do you get your kids to work their brains and build their brains like a muscle?

LESSON NINETEEN

Get your kid a cell phone

It is very hard to learn anything that you don't want to know. And you can't really teach someone that doesn't want to learn. The best way to learn something is to study the things that spark your curiosity. The best way to teach is to wait until your student's curiosity is piqued and then present the answers to his questions in a novel way.

Plato once wrote, "Do not then train youths by force and harshness, but direct them to it by what amuses their minds so that you may be better able to discover with accuracy the peculiar bent of the genius of each."

What I think Plato was trying to say here was that you can't force kids to learn things that they don't want to know. You have to wait until your kid asks a question before you get the opportunity to teach.

One day when my daughter was in 5th grade she came to me and said, "Daddy, I need a cell phone." I thought I had a teachable moment here. I tried to explain the difference between needs and wants. I told her a need is something that you have to have. A need can be something like water. You can't live without water. It can be something like paper and pencils for school. You can't really do your job at school without pencils and paper. It can be soccer cleats. If you want to play soccer, you have to have a good pair of soccer shoes. I told her that we could buy her a new pair of soccer shoes, but we don't buy things that we want. We only buy things that we need.

She said, "I get that, Daddy, but you don't understand. I need a cell phone. Everyone else in my class has a cell phone. I have to get a cell phone. I am a freak, an outcast. I NEED a cell phone."

I persisted, "Wants are more like things that you don't really have to have to live." I told her, "I want a new Porsche. I don't really need a new car, but it would be nice if I had a new Porsche. It would be fun to drive. My friends would all be envious and impressed and I would look really good driving around in a new 911."

I told her, "Every time we go to Costco or Trader Joe's we see things we want. Sometimes we even put these things in the basket. Then, when we get to the checkout line I look at the basket and say to myself, 'Do I really need this or that? Do we really need that fancy blender or this $20 piece of cheese?' If we don't, I put it back. We need to save that money to send you to college, and I would much rather send you to college than to eat a $20 piece of cheese."

She persisted, "Yes, Daddy, but think of it this way. It's a child safety issue. You want me to be safe, right? You want to know where I am and you want me to be able to call you if I need you, right?" I hate it when she uses logic on me. I know that she's smarter than me and she kind of had me. So I got mad. I wasn't really mad. I just pretended to be mad, but in a gruff voice, I said, "You're not getting a cell phone. I'm not paying $30 a month for you to have a phone."

She didn't fluster. She didn't move. She stomped her foot and demanded, "I NEED A CELL PHONE."

Now I was stuck. I was out-maneuvered, out-thought, and out-gunned. She had more passion about this issue than I had resolve. I thought that I had to take another tack. I said, "Ok, ok, how bad do you want a cell phone?" She looked at me and said, "I'll do anything." I said, "Anything?" She said, "Anything."

Now I knew I had something to work with. If she's willing to put in the effort, then I could use this phone thing as a motivational tool, a candy, a carrot to get something that I wanted. I thought at the very least I could wait until school gets out for the summer and maybe stall the advance of technology for another six months.

I stretched my arms and looked around my office. I already knew what I was going to do. I reached behind me and found my old college Algebra textbook. I pulled it out of the bookshelf and handed it to her. I said, "Here, do this. Do every odd problem in this textbook, and I will buy you a cell phone."

She said, "Fine." She took the book and stomped out of the room.

I thought, Holy crap. Did that just happen? Does she really know what she's up against? She's 11 years old. Is she really going to do that?

For the next couple of days, she tried to do the problems in the book. She would call me in every 10 minutes or so and ask me a question on this or that. I would go in and sit with her. We would read through the chapter and do the sample problems. After a couple days of doing this, I realized that this was a really stupid book. The explanations were bad and the example problems didn't match the problems at the end of the chapter. I started looking around for a better textbook.

I was really lucky. I found the perfect book. As it turned out, a friend of ours was writing an Algebra textbook for girls. I'll talk about that later.

Anyway, we got a copy of this book. It was an unbound draft of loose leaf paper in a large three-ring binder. It was great. My daughter and I sat and did the first few chapters together. The book was clear and concise. The sample problems were good and the chapter problems were simple but tricky enough to keep my daughter engaged.

By the time we got the right book and got started on reading it, her school had ended and summer break had begun. I sat with my daughter and showed her how to work. I taught her how to study math. I showed her how to read the chapter, read every word. Do all of the examples. Write them down step by step. Then try the problems in the back. If you run into trouble or you see something that you can't figure out, call me and I will help you.

It's hard to believe, even when I think about it now. It turns out that my daughter is really good at math. She likes the challenge of the tricky problems and she likes the feeling she gets when she solves a problem. I know it sounds crazy, but through the course of the summer my daughter sat in her room and worked on that math book until she finished the whole book. It wasn't easy. She got stuck every once in a while. A couple times she got very emotional. She would freak out and say, "I don't get it, I don't get it. I can't do this. It doesn't make any sense." I was lucky enough to be there when that happened. I would come in and calm her down and explain the problem but –

There was something more to this.

My daughter was trying to make sense of abstract thought for the first time. She wasn't getting it. She thought she was stupid and that these ideas were beyond her. She thought there was some kind of magic, something else that she couldn't know that only smart people knew. She couldn't explain it, but I knew how she felt. I remember feeling the same way. It was like a curtain or a dark sheet of glass in my mind. If I could just see on the other side, I could know the secret knowledge. I thought smart people understood the secret knowledge, but I wasn't smart. I wasn't one of them. I remember freaking out, getting scared and quitting. I didn't do it. I didn't push through the curtain and make myself understand.

Well, I knew how she felt. I tried to break the mood. I tried to shatter the illusion. I told her that there wasn't anything special about this. There wasn't any magic. There wasn't anything that she couldn't learn or couldn't know about this. I told her math is the one thing that she could do. It's like cooking. The recipe is like an equation. You just find the right recipe, find the right ingredients, then plug the ingredients into the equation and solve the problem step by step just like baking a cake.

I told her that she could learn it and that everything she needed to know was in that book. I shattered the illusion by sitting with her and rereading the chapter, stepping through the examples and doing the problems. And after a while, after she calmed down, we went through her problems and found where she made a mistake. We did a few problems until she could do the problems by herself. We worked on it until she got the right answer. And then SMASH. She did it. She broke through the dark glass. She learned that she could do it. This was the major break that made all of the difference.

From there it was all downhill. She worked on the book two or three hours a day through the rest of the summer. Through that summer she sat down and she taught herself Algebra. It was pretty cool.

Here's the thing. I think most girls, and a lot of guys, get to this point and they stop. There's no one there to help them push through. There's no one there to help them break the glass—to shatter the illusion. It's too hard. It's too painful. It's harder to sit down and push through than it is just to say, "Oh honey, I'm sorry, maybe math just isn't your thing." I think this is where girls get stuck and stop thinking about working on harder problems. I think if we could take the time to push through these little problems, we could help a lot of kids break through and learn how to think about bigger things.

Back to the story. The next fall we had moved and she was starting a new school. It was a new house in a new neighborhood, with new people in a different place. Before school, I met with the principal and told her that we should probably put my daughter in Algebra. I told her that she had been homeschooled over the summer and it would be good for her if she could take the class in a classroom just to reconfirm some of the finer points.

Well, the principal wasn't having it. She said, "No, we don't do that. We aren't going to put a sixth-grade girl into an eighth-grade class. Most of the kids in that class are boys and she'll just get picked on." I tried to argue with her for a while, but it didn't work. They wouldn't do it. Disappointed, I got up to leave. On the way out I said one more thing. I said, "You know, it is in your best interest to put her in this Algebra class. I know my daughter and she's not going to get picked on. If anything she's going to do the picking. If she gets bored, she'll get anxious. If she gets anxious, she'll start acting out. When she gets bored, she'll make the teacher's life a living hell. If I were you, I'd put her in Algebra. It will just make things easier for everybody." The principal thanked me for my input and said she would think about it.

By Christmas, they had removed her from her regular math class and placed her into the Algebra class that we wanted. As it turns out, her regular teacher couldn't take it anymore. She said that every time she had made a mistake in class, my daughter would get out of her seat, come to the board, take the chalk and teach the teacher how to do the problem.

So, what's my point here?

My point is that this is an example of how to be a purposeful parent, a Superdaddy. If you want to be a Superdaddy and you have reconfirmed your commitment to making better children, to placing your children as your number one priority, then you have to be there. You have to be there for your kids at the exact moment that they have a question for you to answer.

It is all a timing thing.

Knowing that she was good at something and especially something hard like math gave her the confidence to push through the curtain, break through the dark glass and start to design her own path.

And that one time, the time that I was there to show her that she could do math, changed the direction that her life took. If I hadn't happened to be there just then, she might not have ever figured out that she was good at math. She might have, like so many other little girls, just decided that math wasn't her thing and moved down to the lower rungs of life's ladder.

And to do that you need to be there. Curiosity is fickle. A question is fleeting. A kid might want to know something for only a minute or two. If you're lucky enough to be there when they ask the question, you have an opportunity to teach. The trick is to be there. You need to be there at that moment when your kid wants to know the answer. If you're not there, you have lost that chance and it probably won't come up again.

This is why being a "stay-at-home mom" or "stay-at-home dad" is such a big deal. If you are able to stay at home with your kids, you are giving yourself more time with your kids and you're giving yourself many, many more chances to catch these fleeting teachable moments.

Commit yourself to becoming a purposeful parent and stay at home with your kids. Make the commitment to placing your children as your number one priority, and reconfirm your commitment to making the world a better place by making better children.

You can get your kids to work that hard.

You can get your kids to concentrate on one thing for hours on end.

You can get your kids to work their brains and build their brains like a muscle.

If you use this trick, you can get your kids to study.

If you use this trick, you can make your kids learn.

If they can learn how to focus, they can build their brain into a huge, dense, hardened muscle.

And if they work their brains long enough and hard enough, they will grow to have Super Intelligence.

Superpower #19

Smarts

First things first, being intelligent and being smart are two different things. Having a very high Intelligence Quotient does not guarantee success, fulfillment or happiness.

Yes, having some basic level of intelligence is necessary to make your way in the world, and having a little more intelligence correlates well with greater success, but I know plenty of very intelligent guys that don't consider themselves successful, fulfilled or happy.

Let's unpack this idea a bit more. I use the words "intelligence" and "smarts" in slightly different ways.

I consider an intelligent person to be someone that takes standardized tests well and has a high IQ. Intelligent people have minds that work faster than the average mind; they have better memories and their minds work in different ways.

But in this example, I define "smart" as something different. To be smart a person needs to balance these three independent qualities:

1) Intelligence
2) Time
3) Abstract sources

Intelligence –

To be intelligent, you need a high IQ. You need to get a high score on a standardized test like the ACT or the SAT. You need to have a lot of mental horsepower and you need to be quick. There are a thousand different ways to define intelligence. I think that there is northern intelligence and southern intelligence. I think there is eastern intelligence and western intelligence. I think that there is a different kind of intelligence for each different part of the world, and I think there is a different intelligence for each part of the brain. Some girls are good with numbers, and some guys are good with people. Some people are good with language, and some people are good with abstract thought. Some brains have a really fast processor speed, and some minds have unbelievable memory. If you have been blessed with the natural gift of high intelligence, then be thankful.

Time –

Time is a zero-sum game. If you spend your time doing one thing, you cannot spend that time doing something else. If you spend all of your time watching television or playing video games, you cannot use that time to read and learn from abstract sources. If you spend all of your time working at a job for money, you cannot use that time to learn calculus or economics. The more time you spend learning from abstract sources, the smarter you will be. And if you want to be smart, you have to make painful choices. Because time is a zero-sum game, you will have to choose to spend the limited time that you have learning and not spend that time doing something else. If you are not very intelligent but you take a lot of time to learn, you can become smarter than someone that is very intelligent.

Abstract sources –

An abstract source is accumulated human knowledge. Throughout history, when people have a problem they take a lot of time to figure out a solution to that problem. They might have tried hundreds of things over dozens of years to solve that problem. The reason that technology has advanced so fast is that we as humans don't have to re-invent a new solution to the same problem over and over and over again. All's we have to do is just find the person that has already solved the problem and ask him. Just a dozen years ago it was difficult to find the answer to a question. Now with the internet, anyone in the modern world can find a solution to almost any problem they have.

So to be smart you have to balance these three qualities: intelligence, time and abstract sources.

If you are not that intelligent, you just have to spend more time and learn from abstract sources.

If you don't have enough time, you need to have more intelligence and fast access to good abstract sources.

If you don't have fast access to good abstract sources, you need to be intelligent and have a lot of time to derive solutions from basic principles or re-invent your solutions.

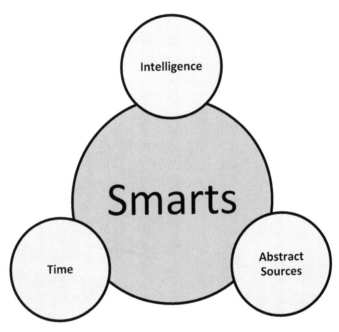

If you are very intelligent but think stupid things or base your schema on faulty logic and incorrect facts, you cannot be smart.

If you are very intelligent but are forced to spend your days hauling water, washing clothes, cooking food or fishing for your family, you cannot be smart.

If you have a lot of time but you smacked your head on the side of a rock while attempting to ski off of a fourteen-thousand-foot cliff in Colorado, you are probably not smart.

If you have a lot of time but you don't have high-speed internet access, you are probably not going to be very smart.

If you have fast access to abstract sources but you use that time to watch porn all day, you are probably not very smart.

So the goal here is to be smart. To be smart you have to balance these three qualities. And you need to teach your kids to balance their intelligence and time and give them access to high-speed abstract sources.

An important thing to remember is that somebody can be really intelligent and still believe really stupid things. And if you are really intelligent and believe in irrational or illogical things, then your schema will not work right. You won't be able to correctly predict the future and you will be unsuccessful, unfulfilled and unhappy.

If you want to become a Superdaddy and raise superhero children, then use the qualities that you have and get smart. It is with this strategy that you and your children can become successful, fulfilled and happy.

Sometime your kids will get hit by something hard.

It might be injury, defeat, disappointment or

something worse. And in this time they will want to

stop, they will want to quit and dwell on their pain.

And sometimes when a person stops, they can fall

backward down a slow, dark spiral of depression.

Wouldn't you like to make your kids stronger, more

resilient and less susceptible to defeat or failure?

Wouldn't it be great if you could find a way to keep

them moving forward?

So they don't stumble?

So they don't fall backward or get depressed?

So they move on to better things and higher places?

LESSON TWENTY

The Multiple Goal Strategy

It's really fun to watch your kids grow up. It's really exciting to see them wake up and become more and more conscious. It is very fulfilling to see them make small progress and then huge leaps of understanding in giant spurts of spiritual growth.

They start off as little bundles of joy with the conceptual capacities of a rabbit. They move through time like the hour hand of a clock, growing so slow that you can't see the change. And then one day BOOM, they say something that just blows you away. You wake up from the drudgery of rearing a baby and realize that they're human. That they're thinking. That they are these small, little creatures and they are already smarter than you—it's overwhelming.

Then they go through a long middle stage of playing and laughing and running and growing. And it's really, really fun.

And then one day they'll have a really bad day where some friends made fun of them, or they missed a shot and lost the game, or they broke their leg and you're in the ER. And you'll want to find a way to console them. One of the hardest things a parent can do is watch their child suffer. The greatest pain I have ever felt was just watching my child cry.

You'll want to do something to stop that. You'll have to do something to end that suffering. You'll be driven by emotions that you have never felt to take this pain and stop your child from hurting.

And what do you do? What can you, as a mere mortal, do to stop the suffering of a child?

But wait. You are not a mere mortal. You are a Superdaddy. You have Superpowers.

Sometimes you can't do anything. Sometimes you just have to let it heal. Sometimes you just have to let time pass and provide some distance from the event. But sometimes there is something you can do.

One of the strategies that we have used to defend against these inevitable very bad days is a multiple goal strategy. We don't let our kids focus on one thing. Sure, they focus on one thing at a time, but they always have at least five things going.

You don't just put them in soccer. You don't just teach them math. You don't just read books with them. You don't just do massive science projects in the backyard. You don't just teach them about music and art. You do all those things, at the same time.

Let's say you're coming up on summertime. Let's say that they'll be getting out of school and they are going to be having a lot of time off. Before that starts you sit with them and pick out five subjects. Five things that they really, really love to do. Or maybe you take three things that they love to do and you pick out two things that they HAVE to do. We usually pick from these five topics:

1. School (grades)
2. Evaluations (test scores)
3. Sports and music (balance)
4. Passions (clubs)
5. Scientific research (backyard projects)

I'm going to break down each of these subjects one by one.

School

It's a sad fact that kids have to work. Kids have to go to school and learn all of this stuff that everyone else knows and everyone else expects them to know. And it's good for them. It's good for them to go to school and learn how to work and how to become disciplined. So school is something that they will need to do and something that they are going to need to become really good at. This is why we put it on the list, and this is why we make it a priority. They need to get good grades in school.

Evaluations

Here we go again. This is a reality of life. Testing is the way the world works. People get tested every day, all the time. The people that learn how to do well in a test situation excel in life and have things a little easier. This is why we put it as a priority. This is why we teach our kids how to take tests and perform well under pressure.

Sports and music

Participating in sports and music and art is all about balance. This is a good life habit for everyone. It's a great habit to teach your kids to not just stay active but become vested in a sport, to participate in a sport and know a sport or to play music and understand music. This keeps your body healthy, your mind strong, and it gives you a sense of community with others that know that sport or play that instrument.

Passions

Finding your passion is a constant pursuit. You should think about it a little bit every day and teach your kids to have it in the back of their mind. Teach them to keep their minds open and recognize their interests and pursue their passions. Encourage them to start a club in school and meet with others that share their same interests. Help them to find their interests and drill down and explore their passions.

Scientific research

I love this. I love doing big, crazy science projects. From building giant Archimedes Death Rays to grill chicken, to building a blast furnace to forge steel, to helping with a two-year project studying the love songs of Australian Finches, to forming a life-sized dinosaur skull out of plaster, I love doing science projects with my kids. It's a great way to spend time with your kids and to teach them the basic understandings of the scientific method.

These are five good subjects. These are the ones we use. You can pick whatever subjects you like. We have picked these subjects because we have learned over time that these five subjects are the five subjects that most colleges and universities evaluate while choosing their freshman class. If you concentrate on these five subjects and build a college application around these five subjects, you will be able to create the strongest possible application. If your student is strong in these five subjects, your student will be able to get into any college or university that they wish.

So now you pick one thing to do from each of these categories. Some of these things are things they need to do and some of these things are stuff they want to do. You combine the two. You sit with them and talk it out. You ask them to think about what they want to do. And then you make a list. You start with the things they want to do. Let's say:

A. They want to learn to fly (#4 from the list).
B. They want to learn to drive a car (#4).
C. They want to spend time with their friends on the beach (#4 and #3).
D. They want to build a blast furnace in the backyard to forge a sword (#5 and #4).

And you know that there are things that you want them to do. These might be things that they know that they need to do and you know that they have to do. These are things like:

X. They have to take a summer school class (#1 from the list).
Y. They have to work out every day to get ready for Cross Country next fall (#3).
Z. They have to start studying for the SATs (#2).

Then you mix them all together and make a grand list. These are the things they are going to do this summer. You make an agreement. You tell them if you do X, Y and Z, I will help you do A, B, C, and D.

You keep them going in at least five directions at once. You help them organize their time and teach them time management. You keep each one of these projects going all of the time.

And here's the kicker. Not only is this a great way to teach your kids about each of these five subjects, not only is this a great way to spend time with your kids and teach them the things in life that you think are important, but it is also a great way to teach your kids how to diversify their interests.

It is a great way to keep them strong. To keep them balanced, to keep them healthy, to keep them happy, and to keep them moving forward.

So now let's go back to the top and talk about these really bad days. Let's say your kid has a really bad day in one of his five subjects. Let's say he breaks his leg playing basketball or she screws up on a chemistry test. Then you can go back and tell them:

"Okay, you had a bad day. This didn't go the way we planned. But that's okay. This isn't the only thing that you've got going on. You've got four other things you're working on. When life zigs, we zag. It is time to refocus. We are going to let that setback or problem rest for a while and concentrate on the next big idea, your next big project."

And then you move on to one of the other four subjects that you have been working on.

This is called "Next Play Focus." You focus on the next play (in volleyball or soccer or whatever) and not the last play. You spend a moment reviewing your past mistakes—but just a moment. Don't waste time feeling bad or running your screw up over and over and over in your mind.

Move on.

This is why we keep at least five different things running all the time. We keep five subjects running so if we hit a bump in one subject we can pivot to the next subject and keep moving forward.

The multiple goal strategy really helps. This is a great way to keep your kids on track and not let them get distracted or depressed or fall down a downward spiral.

And there's something else I've told my kids.

Sometimes really bad things happen. Sometimes really, really bad things happen. This is when someone you love is told they have a terminal illness and gets sick, or someone you know has an accident and is injured beyond repair, or someone very close to you is killed.

Sometimes the pain is so intense, the consequences are so bad that the circumstance changes your life and their lives forever. Sometimes it's out of your control; you didn't have anything to do with it, and it disrupts everything and everyone you know.

Sometimes when they've had really, really bad days, days in which the consequences are so bad that life stops and whatever you were doing seem trivial and unimportant, you have to refocus. And you have to make your kids refocus.

In these times it is important to stop the moment, hold your children a while and love them up.

But just a while—then you need to tell them that they need to refocus and stop focusing on themselves. Ruminating on your own pain and problems is unhealthy and a silly waste of time. It is greedy and selfish to waste time thinking about and focusing on yourself and your problems. You need to pick your head up and look around. You need to think about the world and where you sit on the planet.

And then tell them this –

Listen.

This is important.

Stop messing around.

The world is messed up.

The world needs your help.

We are depending on you to help us fix things and save the world.

We need you to stop screwing around, stop focusing on your pain and your problems.

I need your help.
The world needs your help.
We need you to get back to work.
And become a superhero.
And help us save the world.

This is not a joke. I'm not kidding around here.

We do have the power to make the world better.
We do have the power to save the planet and all of humanity.

There is a way to make your kids stronger.

There is a way you can build a system that makes your kids more resilient.

You can keep them moving forward in times of trouble and struggle and pain.

Sure they will stumble. Sure they will fall.

But not backwards—your kids will fall forwards.

Your kids will move on to better things and higher places.

Become a Superdaddy.

Instigate the multiple goal strategy and keep your kids on track to becoming superheroes.

Superpower #20

Success

What is success and how can success be a Superpower?

In the last chapter, we talked about a strategy that you can use to teach your kids how to become successful. By dividing their energies into different projects, they can mitigate the devastations of setbacks and stumbles. By shifting focus and falling forward, they can stumble from failure to success without wasting mental energies bumming out about something that didn't go the way they planned.

When I was a teenager, I went through the whole nihilism thing.

One night in the ICU of our local hospital I decked our family pastor. As I was being pinned to the wall by hospital security, our pastor grabbed me by the throat and screamed, "YOU ARE GOING TO HELL!"

No shit, I thought. Well, let's get to it then.

That night I came face to face with the hard truth that life is absurd.

I fell away from my belief in God and I gave up on the whole trying-to-be-good thing. I moved to Aspen, Colorado and became a ski bum. I embraced the hedonistic lifestyle. To make money I worked as a bartender and sold cocaine. I skied almost every winter day and partied every night in a dozen different ski resorts around the world for about ten years.

I was desperate and depressed. Moving to a new place is a great diversion. It was fun to change everything. You have to busy yourself with a myriad of trivial tasks. You have to get a new job and find a place to live. You have to meet hundreds of new people. And in all of that newness, you have the opportunity to re-invent yourself. Unrestrained by the expectations and obligations of your friends and family back home, you can create a newer, more complete, more correct version of yourself.

If you ever find yourself desperate and depressed, I highly recommend that you just leave everything you have behind, move halfway around the world and settle into a new place. If you move to a new and different ski resort every year, you can easily divert yourself with newness and diversion over and over and over again for a long, long time. But you are just burning time. You are just diverting yourself away from the things that are ultimately tearing at you.

In that time, over about ten years or so, I found that I was able to find the more complete, more correct version of myself and build myself into a better version of me. But I was still very close to suicide. Thinking back, I was in suicide, a kind of a slow boiling suicide, ingesting every available type, kind and amount of anesthetic and then throwing myself off rocks and cliffs or out of airplanes.

I was consumed, obsessed really, with thoughts of the absurdity of life. I had rejected God and any meaning. I had felt betrayed and lied to by the church and even society. I was having a hard time even understanding reality. I was trying to coalesce together a bundle of different ideas from Christianity to Carlos Castaneda.

I didn't start to read until I was 24. From there it took me a couple years to stumble onto Smith, Dennett, and Nietzsche. It took an even longer time to build context around their ideas.

Light doesn't fill an empty space. If there is nothing in the void, nothing for the light to reflect off of, then the light does not show you anything. You need to have something there. You need to have life's experiences. You need to have done something, experienced suffering, moved through reality for a while to build up your sense of self that the light can bounce off of. You need something inside the void for the light to illuminate.

And so it was for me.

Nietzsche's Beyond Good and Evil saved my life. I'm not sure where I was. It was probably Cameroon, but it might have been Honolulu. It was Nietzsche's realization—no, more like an explanation that life was absurd that changed my life. Fred was saying things that I already knew from my experiences but had never really seen before he turned on the light.

I mean, you really have to ingest a lot of other ideas before you can get to this point. You have to decide. You have to choose. You have to choose to believe that you do have a choice, that you do have free will. That you can understand and accept the fact that life is painful and pointless and then still continue to live. You can step outside of yourself and look back at yourself at the fool that is you. And laugh.

But then you have to choose. You have to choose free will, and then you have to choose to live. And then you have to decide what is worth living for. You have to choose your values. And then you have to choose your purpose. And then you have to choose your meaning.

And you can. You can because you can. You can because you are going to have to choose anyway and you might as well choose the thing that gives you more choice, more freedom.

So, I chose. I chose to believe that life has meaning. I chose to believe that life has the meaning that you choose to give it. You can choose to give life meaning and you can choose the meaning that you give life.

Here is what I have chosen;
I believe that I have free will.
I believe that I have the power to design my life.
I believe that life has meaning and that I have the power to define that meaning.
I believe that I have a purpose and that I have the power to define that purpose.
I believe that the goal of life is to be happy.
But happiness is not something that you can just conjure.
To be happy, you have to be fulfilled.
To be fulfilled, you have to successfully accomplish something.
Success comes from years and years of hard work and suffering in pursuit of a goal.
So to be happy you need to define your values.
Then use those values to design your purpose.
Then understanding your purpose, you choose a goal.
Choose a goal that makes the world a better place.
Choose a goal that improves the lives of your fellow humans.

Choose the most difficult and complicated goal you can possibly imagine.

Then get to work.

After many, many years you will successfully accomplish your goal.

With that success, you will become fulfilled.

And with fulfillment, you will become happy.

Success is the Superpower that leads to happiness. And implementing this system will lead to success.

And becoming successful will lead to happiness.

I didn't really understand this until I was—well, until just now.

This year I will turn 60.

If I could have found my way through this maze of ideas when I was, say, 30, I would have had a completely different life.

If you can find your way through this maze, you can find happiness. And the sooner you start, the better your chances will be.

And if you can give your children these ideas, you can help them find happiness.

EPILOGUE

So why did I write this book?

I wrote this book because I see all around me fathers that have never learned how to be fathers.

I see guys fumbling to reinvent solutions to problems within their families that are thousands of years old.

And I see men struggling to balance between the natural urges of being a father and the ridiculous expectations of a media-driven life.

I see my place on this earth and my place on life's timeline.

I feel the weight and the burden of empathy.

I place my pain on my life map and understand how that pain moved me to where I stand now.

I know that because of my suffering I have discovered a very specific set of solutions to a universal set of problems.

I have faced this common set of problems and have spent dozens of years discovering and inventing and improving the solutions to the problems of raising a family. I figured that if I could compile a set of solutions (abstract sources), I might be able to shorten the time that an average father would need to learn how to raise his kids.

This would make his life and the lives of his loved ones better.

About ten years ago while sitting in my car stopped in a traffic jam on the "I-5", melted to my seat, slithering home, fired, beaten, and depressed, I had an epiphany.

I thought about where I was and where I was going.

I had known for a while that my life hadn't been moving in a direction that felt right. I knew that I had been taking time away from the things that I valued most and spent it on fulfilling obligations imposed on me from things that I didn't really care about. I felt bad for my kids and I felt bad for my wife. I felt guilty for not being there with them and I felt rotten from not being there for them.

I thought about Friedrich, Matt, Mark and John and the lessons that I had forgotten.

I decided to think about my values.

I decided to take this time to reevaluate, reorganize and reprioritize the things that I valued most and build my life around those values.

I felt bad for my kids, but I knew I could change that. I felt bad for my wife, and I knew I could change that too.

I thought that maybe me being fired wasn't such a bad thing. I thought that maybe I could make this work.

If my goal was to have a happy, successful family, I wondered if it would be possible to start with the goal and work backward. I thought that I could start with the product—the idea of having a happy, successful family—and reverse engineer a solution. Instead of working my whole life to make enough money to be able to buy the time I would need to form better relationships with my kids, I could just spend the time I had now to make better relationships with my wife and my kids.

And this brought me back to the big questions: What do I value? What is important to me? Life is a zero-sum game. You only get so many hours in one life to live, and you need to make sure that you decide for yourself what you spend those hours doing. You only have a limited amount of time, so it is in your best interest to prioritize your time, set your values and spend the most amount of your time on the things that you value most.

So that's what I did.

I went home and packed the car. I took my wife and kids on a wild adventure. We went for a month driving and camping across the country. I took that time to think things through and reset my values.

Once I had my values set and prioritized, I defined my purpose.

I understood Maslow's hierarchy of needs and I realized that I had already achieved the first three levels of his pyramid. I mean, we live in a First World, right? Most of this lower level stuff has been given to us by our parents.

After a long and calm period of contemplation, I chose to ignore the fourth level, esteem (i.e., concerning myself with what other people think of me). I realized that if I were to employ a strategy of seeking the respect or admiration from people outside of myself, I would be going against one of my core values—self-reliance. So I decided not to care about what other people thought of me and moved on to the top of the pyramid.

There are two levels above esteem: self-actualization, to reach your full potential, to be all that you can be; and transcendence, giving oneself to a higher goal. I liked these ideas. They spoke more to a process, a constant rate of change, a continual path to improvement.

Self-actualization, "What a man can be, he must be." The idea is to leverage your strengths to maximize your achievements, to work as hard as you possibly can to do as much as you can to reach your full potential. It seemed to me that one could never really reach one's full potential. Reaching your full potential would be something that you could continually strive for.

And then there is transcendence. This is another good one. For me transcendence means finding a higher purpose; it means trying to find a way to make the world a better place for everyone.

I think that it is possible to combine these last two levels into one changing, moving, evolving goal. The goal is to find a way to leverage your strengths, to work as hard as you can at doing something that will make the world a better place.

So that is what I decided to do. I decided that I wanted to try and make the world a better place.

I took an accounting of some of the problems that I saw before me and the problems that I saw amongst the other fathers that I knew. And then I decided to try and solve these problems.

So, that is why I wrote this book.

I believe that;

The cornerstone of society

is the family

and the foundation of the family is

fatherhood

And I want to find a way to make better fathers. That is my goal. That is my task.

Being a parent is a humbling job. It is difficult and dangerous and takes a tremendous amount of work.

So, why do this? Why have kids? Why invest your time and your life raising children?

Because of Earthbound Life

Because of Human Brains

Because of Newton's Second Law and

Because having a Strong Family is one of the most valuable things you can have.

Raising better children is the purpose and meaning of life.

And you can become a real superhero in the real world. Not some kind of fantasy or imaginary character in a movie or a comic book, but a real, live superhero with real, live Superpowers.

You can change the world.

You can make the world a better place.

You don't need to be rich or powerful.

You just need the time and the resources that you have in front of you right now to change the destiny of you, your kids, your family, your future, your community, your country, and the world by changing your values and dedicating your time to becoming a purposeful parent and raising better children.

Where is Superman?

Where are the superheroes?

Where are the people that we are going to need to step in in the moment of crisis and save the world?

They are standing right in front of you staring in the mirror.

You can be a purposeful parent.

You can be a Superdaddy.

You can raise superheroes.

And save the world.

Start now.

If you have enjoyed *How to Raise a Superhero* please go to Amazon and take a moment to leave an honest review.

Help spread the word. Share this book with your friends, family and other guys that you know that are about to become fathers. It will help men find meaning in their lives and that will help make the world a better place.